# TO BURY THE DEAD

# TO BURY THE DEAD

IGNACIO MARTÍNEZ DE PISÓN

TRANSLATED FROM THE SPANISH
BY ANNE McLEAN

Carnival

Parthian
The Old Surgery
Napier Street
Cardigan
SA43 1ED
www.parthianbooks.co.uk
www.carnivalpublishing.co.uk

Published with the financial support of
the Welsh Books Council.

First published in Spanish in 2005 as *Enterrar a los muertos*
by Seix Barral, S.A., Barcelona.
First published in Great Britain in 2009 by Parthian.



The publication of this work has been made possible through a subsidy received from the Directorate General for Books, Archives and Libraries of the Spanish Ministry of Culture.

ISBN 978-1-905762-41-5

Editor: Laura Baker

Cover design: www.theundercard.co.uk
Cover image: © Getty Images

Typeset by logodædaly

Printed and bound by Gwasg Gomer, Llandysul, Wales

British Library Cataloguing in Publication Data

A cataloguing record for this book is available from the British Library.

**Ignacio Martínez de Pisón** was born in Zaragoza in 1960 and has lived in Barcelona since 1982. He is the author of a dozen books, notably the short story collection *El fin de los buenos tiempos* (1994, *Last of the Good Times*) and novels *Carreteras secundarias* (1996, *Back Roads*) and *Dientes de leche* (2008, *Milk Teeth*). He has also compiled a sort of collective novel called *Partes de guerra* (2009), an anthology of Spanish Civil War stories by writers of a wide range of generations, ideologies and styles.

*To Bury the Dead* was awarded the International Rodolfo Walsh Prize for Non-fiction and the Dulce Chacón Prize for Spanish Narrative in 2006.

**Anne McLean** translates Spanish and Latin American novels, short stories, memoirs and other writings by authors including Julio Cortázar, Juan Gabriel Vásquez, Enrique Vila-Matas and Héctor Abad Faciolince. Her translations of novels by Javier Cercas have been short-listed for the IMPAC prize and awarded the Premio Valle Inclán and the Independent Foreign Fiction Prize.

# TO BURY THE DEAD

# CONTENTS

I first heard of José Robles Pazos in a book from the late 1970s called *John Dos Passos: Rocinante Loses His Way*. Taking the novelist's own writing as his starting point, the Argentinian author Héctor Baggio recreated Dos Passos' relationship with Spain up to the Civil War, which would be such a decisive factor in his life and work. The character of Robles in that book was a slightly blurred, secondary figure, and only his unfortunate end would finally grant the tale of his friendship with Dos Passos an unexpected importance. Curiosity led me to track this friendship through further readings. I searched for other testimonies and news, which in turn led to more testimonies and more news, and at some point I had the feeling it was they who were coming to find me, searching me out. By then that initial curiosity had already become an obsession, and one day I found myself trying to reconstruct the story from the beginning, from the time Dos Passos and Robles met for the first time in the winter of 1916.

# 1

In 1916 Pepe Robles was nineteen years old and studying Philosophy and Literature at the University of Madrid. Though born in Santiago de Compostela, he grew up in the Madrid, where his father, an occasional translator of Galician poetry, worked as an archivist. As a student his finances must have been quite precarious, but once in a while he allowed himself a short trip to one of the surrounding cities. On an excursion to Toledo in a third-class carriage he struck up a conversation with a North American just a year older than him. They spoke of painting

and poetry, and then they went together to admire El Greco's *The Burial of the Count of Orgaz*. A friendship developed between them almost immediately. They shared a love of travel and cultural interests and, while Robles was trying to improve his English, Dos Passos was trying to do the same with his Spanish. They were also drawn together by the academic circles in which they both moved. The *Residencia de Estudiantes* and the *Centro de Estudios Históricos*, which would both soon be important in Robles' life, already were in that of Dos Passos, who, while waiting for a vacancy in the Student Residence, was renting a room near the Puerta del Sol and, in the meantime, attending Spanish language and literature courses at the Centre for Historical Studies.

Only Robles' death would end this friendship. In *The Theme Is Freedom*, Dos Passos saw him as 'a man of vigorous, skeptical, and inquiring mind.' In *The Best Times*, his book of memoirs written half a century after that first encounter, he described him as having 'a sharper tongue than my educationist and liberal acquaintances. He laughed at everything. His talk was more like Pío Baroja's tart writing.' So, while for them bullfights were taboo, Dos Passos remembers how much Robles enjoyed going to the bullring and sketching the toreros. Robles was also a good travel companion. He and Dos Passos had time to make other excursions together before, towards the end of January, the American received a telegram at the Student Residence informing him of the death of his father and had to pack his bags to return to the United States. Dos Passos left in such a rush that he couldn't even say goodbye to his friend in person, and eventually did so by letter from on board the *Touraine*. In that letter, the first of many that he

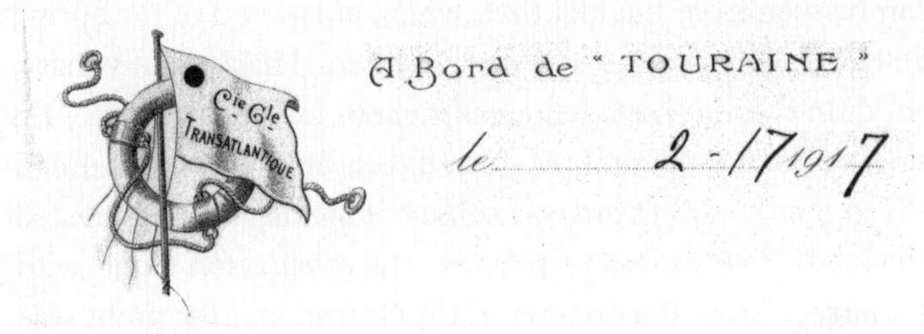


would write to Robles and the only one of them written in French, he announced his desire to return as soon as possible to Spain, a country by which he felt '*vraiment fasciné*.'

In 1918, after graduating with a final-year dissertation on the proverbs contained in Cervantes' *Persiles*, José Robles began work as a professor of Spanish literature in the school attached to the Residencia. During the two following terms he combined teaching with a part-time position at the Centre for Historical Studies. The personal satisfaction both these

activities yielded must have been greater than the economic benefits. Evidence of his financial difficulties in those years can be seen from the fact that, when, at the end of the spring of 1920, he was offered a post at Johns Hopkins University, he didn't even have enough money for the voyage. He applied to the Committee for Higher Studies on 12 June, 'given that he didn't possess sufficient means,' and requested a grant of two thousand pesetas. His application came with a reference from the director of the Centre, and the grant was awarded on 5 July.

The previous year José Robles had married Márgara Villegas, a student at San Fernando School of Fine Arts, which was attached to the *Institución Libre de Enseñanza*. They made a handsome couple: he was tall, dark and good-looking; she was a petite brunette, with a round face and sweet expression. Márgara was the sister of Amparo Villegas, a well-known actress of the day, and thanks to her invitations the young couple were often able to attend the

theatre free. Sometimes they went with their good friend Maurice Coindreau, who was then studying at the University of Madrid and a few years later would translate books by Ramón del Valle-Inclán and Dos Passos into French. It was through Pepe Robles that Coindreau met these authors. The Frenchman recalled his first encounter with the latter in a series of interviews for *France-Culture* later published under the title *Mémoires d'un traducteur*. It took place in the library of the Ateneo. Robles pointed out a 'big, gangling youth who looked nothing like a Madrileño' and told him he was a man who was always coming and going. According to Coindreau, when Robles applied for a position as professor at Johns Hopkins 'it wasn't so much to earn more money as to get to know the United States and be reunited with his friend Dos Passos.'

In March 1920, while awaiting a reply from Johns Hopkins, Márgara and Pepe had their first baby, Francisco (who was always known as Coco). At the end of that summer they moved to Baltimore. Initially contracted as a Spanish language instructor, Robles would be promoted in 1922 to associate professor. During those first years in the United States, Robles and Dos Passos corresponded with great frequency, having resumed their friendship at the end of 1919 and beginning of 1920 in Spain. In one of these letters, Dos Passos expressed his happiness at the news of Robles' appointment and offered to show the family around 'the new Babylon.' In another, he described Baltimore as '*una población muy provincial* [sic], *muy típica, muy aburrida*,' whose inhabitants were famous for their hospitality.

In February 1924, in very parochial, very typical and very boring Baltimore the couple's second child was born. Her godfather would be Maurice Coindreau, who had begun

teaching at Princeton University. They named the little girl Margarita, though from the start they called her Miggie, after an opera singer they'd met on one of their Atlantic crossings. They were then living in a modest house on Maryland Avenue but, as soon as their economic situation allowed, they moved to a slightly larger place on 25th Street. Their first years in North America passed calmly, bringing up their children and fulfilling academic obligations, while Pepe devoted his free time to playing the piano and studying Russian, in order to read the Russian classics in the original.

Judging from his correspondence with John Dos Passos, who was familiarly known as Dos, in the twenties Pepe Robles was not lacking in literary ambitions of his own. He'd been working on a novel for some time ('my interminable novel') and had written several poems and a play he dreamed would open one day in Madrid. In his letters, Dos praised the fragments Pepe gave him to read, and told him of his financial predicaments and his illnesses, his travels and his difficulties in finding a place to live in New York and of his own progress as a writer. Dos also commented on his current reading, showing that his interest in the contemporary Spanish cultural scene was still keen: in a letter of 1924 he asked about Unamuno's exile to Fuerteventura, in another, from 1926, he expressed his enthusiasm for *Los cuernos de Don Friolera* by Valle-Inclán, an author whose previous works he 'hadn't liked much.' Perhaps most surprising is that, as early as 1924, he'd read 'a book of poetry by an Argentine, Jorge Luis Borges, which I thought good, although rather heavy and metaphysical.'

Dos Passos' letters also reflect the Robles' domestic situation, such as Márgara's delicate state of health shortly before Miggie's birth or Coco's appendectomy in 1926. With respect to this surgery he joked: 'You're going to have to start writing comedies like the Quintero brothers and get rich if your children keep going in for operations. This year stomach ulcers are the height of chic.'

Between April 1927 and January 1928, Pepe Robles contributed to *La Gaceta Literaria*, which was then the most important journal for young Spanish writers (and for a few foreign hispanophiles, like Coindreau). In *The Literary Gazette* Robles was responsible for a section called 'Yankee Books,' where, often accompanied by his own illustrations,

he reported on the current American literary scene. His first reviews, from April and June 1927, were devoted to *Manhattan Transfer* by Dos Passos and *Fiesta* (*The Sun Also Rises*) by Ernest Hemingway, and these were almost certainly the first published comments in Spain on the work of both writers.

The Robles family usually spent the long university vacations in Madrid. They travelled from Baltimore to New York, where they stayed in Dos' apartment, and from there they embarked on a transatlantic steamer that would take them to the port of Vigo or to Le Havre. On the way back they'd also stay with Dos. They sometimes coincided in his apartment with Maurice Coindreau, who shortly after the publication of *Manhattan Transfer* was already working on its French translation and frequently came to New York to consult with the author. It is quite possible that it was during one of these encounters that Pepe and Márgara conceived the idea of translating Dos' books into Spanish. At the end of the decade they dedicated part of their time to this task. While Pepe worked on his version of *Manhattan Transfer*, Dos Passos' most representative novel, Márgara translated *Rosinante to the Road Again*, a collection of texts in which the American writer recreated his first journeys around Spain.

Both books would be published by the recently created, distinctly left-wing publishing house Cenit. That same publisher included on its list the other translations the couple produced during those years: Márgara did three now-forgotten novels by Michael Gold, Julia Peterkin and Edwin Seaver, and Pepe translated *Babbitt* by Sinclair Lewis. They were soon printing a second edition of *Manhattan Transfer*, which included a translator's prologue. In it Robles Pazos, as well as demonstrating a profound knowledge of the literary work of Dos Passos, portrayed his friend as 'six feet tall, gangly and near sighted,' a curious and indefatigable traveller, a 'radical to the marrow' who sympathized with the causes of the left.

Robles too, although he never joined any political organization, was a man of the left. His fervent republicanism, in fact, had distanced him from the monarchical and conservative part of his family. Alfonso XIII's departure from Spain and the resulting proclamation of the Second Republic in 1931 were undoubtedly met with genuine rejoicing in the Robles' home in Baltimore. That summer the family travelled to the newly Republican Spain, and, through a Jewish acquaintance called José Estrugo he had met in the United States, Robles struck up a friendship with the writer Francisco Ayala, who had published a review of *Manhattan Transfer* in the *Revista de Occidente*. Ayala, Estrugo, Robles and their families all went together to visit Toledo. In his memoirs, Ayala recalls Robles' 'quick and open laugh and a look that reflected his innocent goodness.'

Robles Pazos took a sabbatical for the academic year of 1931-1932, which he and his family spent in Madrid. They

lived in a rented flat near the bullring on the Carretera de Aragón, where, at that time and until its closure in 1934, they still held bullfights: in fact, they could see them from their window. Pepe Robles, a talkative and lively man, a good friend to his friends, enjoyed the *tertulias* or cultural gatherings in the cafés. 'There is nothing more fruitful than wasting time, and no better place for wasting time than a café,' he would write a few years later. His theory on *tertulias* goes further: 'The café is the refuge of sincerity. Social conventions oblige us to live a more or less fictitious life all day long, but when it comes time for the *tertulia*, always eagerly anticipated, then we can let loose every truth that occurs to us.'

Pepe usually went to the cafés alone, though sometimes Márgara accompanied him, and on those occasions they left Coco and Miggie in the care of a nanny. Of the various *tertulias*, the one Pepe attended most often was the one at La Granja del Henar, on Calle Alcalá. There he made friends with writers like Valle-Inclán, León Felipe and Ramón J. Sender, with whom, when time allowed, he shared a table on the terrace of the café. The conversation frequently continued at the Robles' flat. In their living room it was not unusual to find Valle-Inclán (whom Robles had to help out financially on more than one occasion) and León Felipe (who aspired to a lectureship in some North American university and would later exchange letters with Pepe asking for advice), but also poets like Rafael Alberti, translators like Wenceslao Roces or such publishers as Rafael Giménez Siles, founder-owner of Cenit.

At that time, Dos Passos kept up his now well-known habits as an inveterate traveller. Though in 1930 he had set up home in Provincetown, Massachusetts, he never passed up a chance to set out with his wife for Europe or Central America. Another of his favourite destinations was Key West, Florida, where he would usually meet up with Ernest Hemingway, one of his best friends at that time. In Key West, through Hemingway, he'd met Katy Smith in 1928; they married a year later and would be together until her death in a traffic accident almost twenty years later.

Back in the United States after his sabbatical, Robles rented a cottage in Provincetown for the 1932 summer holidays. It had a small garden and was close to the beach and to Dos Passos' house. So, for Pepe Robles, that was a summer of long nocturnal *tertulias* with Dos Passos and

Katy, around whom the small colony of writers and artists congregated. Among them was the most illustrious literary critic of the time, Edmund Wilson, who often spent time in an old house down by the port. As well as social gatherings, Wilson devoted the summer to writing the play *Beppo and Beth* and to an extramarital adventure in the absence of Margaret, his second wife (who was to die as the result of an accidental fall in September of that same year). Wilson's annotations in his diaries allow one to imagine how the Robles spent those holidays: strolls to the Long Point lighthouse, picnics on the beach, outings at sea with the fishermen of Truro, attendance perhaps at the local tennis tournament... Although these diaries do not mention Robles by name, he does appear occasionally in the collected letters: in a letter to the writer, editor and critic Malcolm Cowley in January 1940, Wilson writes: 'When I knew him, his left position was quite clear, and he was certainly a man of excellent character.' Robles' friendship with Dos continued to grow closer and, when he visited, what most amused the children was Dos' constant absentmindedness: on one occasion he forgot a slice of cheese between the pages of a book.

Dos' constant wandering meant that his relationship with Robles was frequently an epistolary one, and almost all the letters that survive from the period announce future encounters in Baltimore or New York. For financial reasons, his travels were restricted at the beginning of 1933. While planning more trips away from the United States, Dos Passos visited the Robles family in Baltimore at the end of January. They saw each other again two months later, when the novelist accompanied Katy to Baltimore, where she was having her tonsils removed. The choice of Baltimore as the place for the surgery was influenced by the fact that Dos' old friend Dr Horsley Gantt had joined the staff at Johns Hopkins University as a professor. The operation went ahead without complications, but Katy's recuperation coincided with one of Dos Passos' frequent bouts of rheumatic fever, which forced him into the hospital bed she'd just left free. He remained in hospital for several weeks, which he devoted to reading *Remembrance of Things Past* and to cultivating some of his friendships. Among those who visited him was Robles, as well as Edmund Wilson and Francis Scott Fitzgerald, whose wife, Zelda, was being treated by Adolph Meyer, a colleague of Gantt's. Hemingway would come into contact with Pepe very soon afterwards, during the summer, which they and Dos and Katy spent in Spain.

The Robles now lived on the second floor of a three-storey house at 3221 Guilford Avenue, very close to the university. Their great joy was still returning to Madrid for the holidays. In the summer of 1934 they made an exception, because a Mexican university contracted Pepe to teach a course on Spanish literature. The family travelled on board the *Morro Castle*, a ship that sailed from New York to Havana and Veracruz. When the course was finished, they were meant to return to Baltimore on the same ship, but at the last moment they decided to travel by land to enjoy the scenery. That decision possibly saved their lives. They arrived at the border by train and caught a Greyhound bus there that made numerous stops. During one of them Pepe got out to stretch his legs and buy cigarettes. A little while later, his wife and children saw him return with a shocked expression on his face. He had just learned that in the early hours of that very day, 8 September, fire had destroyed the *Morro Castle* off the coast of New Jersey. The final death toll would reach one hundred and thirty-four.

At the end of that year and the beginning of the next, Dos Passos, again suffering from rheumatic fever, spent some months with Katy in Key West. From there he wrote several letters to Pepe Robles in which he told of his recent experience as a screenwriter for Josef von Sternberg's *The Devil is a Woman* ('it's not worth the trouble of spending the days elaborating idiotic Spanish clichés for Marlene Dietrich'), and encouraged him to visit with his family. It seems that visit never happened, perhaps due to Robles' duties at the university, which then involved teaching as well as academic research.

Robles' scholarly side had led him to specialize in classical Spanish theatre. In 1935, he published an anthology of Lope de Vega's *Cancionero teatral* with Johns Hopkins University Press, as well as an article in the journal *Modern Language Notes* regarding the date of the composition of the play *Fuenteovejuna*. In January of the same year a less ambitious but also more entertaining little book appeared. This was *Cartilla española*, a collection of texts in Spanish, with exercises and vocabulary lists, designed for North American students of the language. The volume set out a delightful journey through Spanish customs, history and culture, and its illustrations, Robles' own, prove his facility for the lively and confident line that Dos Passos had noted twenty years earlier.

The reception of *Cartilla española* was favourable enough to encourage Robles to prepare another similar volume. Its slightly nostalgic title was to be *Tertulias españolas*. The text and drawings were already finished by the spring of 1936, but José Robles would never get to see this book in print. At the beginning of June, as in previous years, he closed up the house on Guilford Avenue and travelled to Spain with his family to enjoy the vacation. They normally rented an apartment in Madrid for the summer months, but that year a good friend who was out of the city lent them his flat on Calle Menéndez y Pelayo. In Robles' luggage he had the original text and drawings, to which he intended to add the necessary vocabulary and exercise sections. The outbreak of the Civil War prevented him from doing so. After his arrest, in December of that year, Márgara Villegas conserved the manuscript intact. Recovered by a professor at the University of Cincinnati and completed by another from Princeton, it was published as 'a tribute to the gallant and cherished author of *Cartilla española*.' It was perhaps no coincidence that the prologue to the volume, by F. Courtney Tarr, is dated 14 April 1938, the seventh anniversary of the proclamation of the Second Republic, a detail that would undoubtedly have pleased the book's author.

What had become of Robles Pazos? When the military launched its attempt to overthrow the Republic, he obtained a leave of absence from Johns Hopkins in order to remain in Spain and offer his services to the legitimate government. In need of external aid and virtually abandoned from the early days by the European powers, the Republican government received the first Soviet military advisors during the month of August. Their commanding officer was Yan Berzin, who up till then had directed the military intelligence service (GRU). Prominent among them was the figure of General Vladimir Gorev, military attaché and chief agent of the GRU in Madrid. With the advisors came a large group of interpreters. Adelina Abramson, a Russian-Argentinian, formed part of that group, and in her book *Mosaico roto* (*Broken Mosaic*), written in collaboration with her sister Paulina, she puts the eventual number of translators sent by Moscow at two hundred and four. A few of their names have survived, for various reasons: Benjamín Abramson (Paulina and Adelina's father), Elizaveta Parshina (author of a memoir called *The Brigadista*) and Sofía Bessmertnaia (killed at Brunete).

However, the historian Daniel Kowalsky has pointed out that, of the almost four hundred Soviet personnel in Spain at the beginning of November 1936, only fourteen were translators. The lack of communication between some of the Russian military officials and their Republican colleagues led to many absurd situations. While in Moscow, the future interpreters, many of them barely familiar with the Spanish language, were receiving intensive courses and preparing to leave for Spain; in Madrid they tried to solve the problem by resorting to translators who were already there. Among these were Abramson, Lydia Kúper (later responsible for a much-praised Spanish translation of *War and Peace*) and José Robles, who, as we know, had some knowledge of Russian.

General Vladimir Gorev spoke English and French. During most of the fifteen months he spent in Spain, his regular interpreter (who, according to the Abramson sisters, was also his lover) was Emma Wolf. But, before she arrived, Pepe Robles served as his interpreter, obliging him to spend a lot of time at the main headquarters of the Soviet advisors, installed first in the Hotel Alfonso, on Gran Vía, and later in the Palace, on the Plaza de las Cortes. On headed notepaper from the second hotel, Robles wrote a couple of letters to Henry Carrington Lancaster, head of the department of Romance Languages at Johns Hopkins University, in which he attempted to allay his fears about the situation of the Republic: 'Do not believe the exaggerations of the fascists' propaganda. We are fine and this thing will be put right.'

A calm and untroubled man, inveterate pipe smoker, Vladimir Gorev enjoyed the sympathy of the people of Madrid and had indisputable military prestige: barely forty

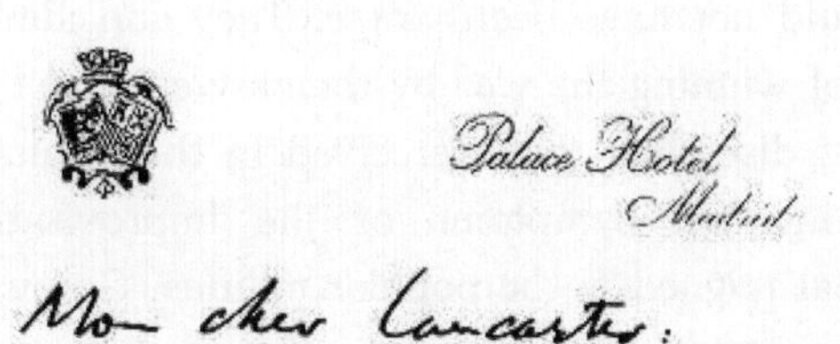


years old, he was the youngest general in the Red Army. The writer Arturo Barea described him in *The Forging of a Rebel* as ‘fair, tall, and strong, with high cheek-bones, frigid blue eyes,’ correct in his treatment of Spanish officials but ruthlessly detached and cold in the discussion of military matters. Although the activities of the Soviet advisors took place mainly in the Palace, Gorev also had an office in the Palacio de Buenavista, headquarters of the War Ministry located at the intersection of Alcalá and Recoletos, and was in constant communication with *comandante* Manuel Estrada, Chief of Staff. Among the secret documents declassified after the collapse of the Soviet Union was a report by André Marty, the organizer of the International Brigades, describing the atmosphere of the Ministry, where anyone could enter ‘without being stopped or searched.’ To Marty’s disgust, the reception area saw a continuous coming and going of visiting officers, unionized workers who cheerfully talked of confidential matters, bureaucrats dictating to typists all over the place, and he was scandalized to see that the women of Socorro Rojo entered the office of the minister, Largo Caballero, without asking for permission.

The Soviet advisors’ opinion of the Republican military

officers could not have been worse. They considered them incapable of winning the war by themselves, and the chaos and lack of discipline they perceived in the ministry itself were nothing but symptoms of the improvisation and disorder that reigned in the popular militias. Gorev was not alone. In the reports (signed with his nom de guerre: Sancho) that he sent to Moscow, he spoke clearly of the suspicions aroused by Estrada and, especially, General Asensio, undersecretary of the War Ministry and Commander in Chief of the central front. He suspected the latter, who was protected by Largo Caballero, of receiving instructions from Franco and thought that, even if he one day managed to remove him from the headquarters of the General Staff, things could only get worse. In any case, the constant disputes between Estrada and Asensio did not benefit the Republic, and the Soviet military officers, anxious to reduce Largo Caballero's power, very soon began a siege against his right-hand man.

Small conspiracies and the duties of his position kept Gorev so busy that his workday lasted from midday until well into the early hours of the morning, which very often prevented him from getting to the front. Some of the routine matters he delegated to Yosif Ratner, military attaché who worked half days at the General Staff and whom his colleagues knew as Juan. Gorev entrusted other tasks to Robles Pazos, who, for example, dealt with the American military attaché on his behalf when he paid a call to request information. Robles held the rank of lieutenant colonel, but he thought like a civilian and always dressed as one, a detail that could only displease those who, like André Marty, considered it a disgrace that the Minister of War's secretary was not a soldier but a union worker. Suspicions were also raised by the fact that Pepe's brother Ramón, an army officer who in the 1960s would become Commander in Chief of the 9th Military Region, had refused to collaborate with the militias, despite the fact that he was in Madrid at the time of the uprising.

At the beginning of November 1936, Franco's troops had reached the banks of the River Manzanares, and the fall of Madrid, under continuous bombardment, seemed imminent. On the fourth of the month, the Council of Ministers decided to transfer the government to Valencia. Four days later, the ministers were already in the new capital of the Republic and their closest collaborators prepared to vacate their Madrid offices as quickly as possible. The socialist Julián Zugazagoitia left a written description of the conditions under which they carried out the evacuation of the Ministry of War, with orderlies who, fearing the enemy would surprise them at work, 'emptied filing cabinets, carried drawers, moved desks and took fright at the news, bad and worse, that arrived from the front.' Undoubtedly José Robles was in the midst of all that intense activity. His friends had advised him from the start to take his family back to the United States, where they would be out of danger and he would be more useful to the Republican cause; but he thought his place was in Spain and, accompanied by his son, he followed his superiors to Valencia.

On their way to the new capital of the Republic, José and Coco Robles took a detour to Alicante to pick up Márgara and Miggie. For reasons of safety many Madrileños had sent their families to the then tranquil city. Pepe's wife and daughter stayed in Alicante from the end of August, and coincided in the Hotel Samper with the children of the bullfighter Belmonte and with Rómulo Negrín, son of the Finance Minister. When Pepe and his family finally arrived in Valencia, the deluge of evacuees and civil servants that accompanied the government was such that, according to some sources, the population of the city had tripled. There was not enough housing for so many people, and the recent arrivals had to make do with finding places to stay in villages up to twenty kilometres from the centre, or crowd together in flats abandoned by their owners. In those early days, the Robles were taken in by a local family.

In Valencia, José Robles worked as a translator at the War Ministry and at the Soviet Embassy, which had installed itself in the Hotel Metropol, right across the street from the bullring. After lunch he usually went to the Ideal Room, on the busy corner of Paz and Comedias, near the old Hotel Palace, which had been converted into an arts centre. Max Aub described the café briefly: 'The pedestal tables with pale marble tops, the floor tiled in black and white, the mirrors covering the walls, the fans hanging from the ceiling,' and Esteban Salazar Chapela wrote: 'Walking into the Ideal Room in the afternoon was not like walking into La Granja or the Lyon or the Regina, literary and artistic cafés of Madrid; it was like walking into all three of those cafés at once, for in the Ideal Room one always met members of each of their circles.' The main Madrid *tertulias* all meeting in the same place: what more could someone like

Pepe Robles hope for? Many intellectuals and artists arranged to meet in the Ideal Room. Among them were some of Robles' old friends: León Felipe, whom Salazar Chapela met again and again on the Calle de la Paz, Francisco Ayala, who was in Valencia due to his position in the secretariat of Álvarez del Vayo's ministry, or Rafael Alberti, who frequently travelled to the city and had traded his poet's beret and cravat for the militiamen's coveralls and espadrilles. Many foreign correspondents and members of the diplomatic missions would also often get together at the Ideal Room, and it seems that Pepe Robles was friendly with, among others, Herbert Matthews of *The New York Times* and the cultural attaché of the American Embassy. In his memoirs, Ayala recalls that, one afternoon at the beginning of December, Robles didn't show up at the *tertulia* and he never saw him again. The image that remained etched in the writer's head was that of an anguished Márgara Villegas who, with her two children by the hand, went 'from one place to another, asking, checking, inquiring, always without the slightest result.'

The previous night the Robles family had just finished dinner with their hosts, and Pepe had settled down to read a book of short stories by Edgar Allan Poe, when there was a knock at the door. A group of men in civilian clothes came into the living room. Without giving any explanation or listening to any pleas, they ordered José to get his coat and come with them.

The next day, as Ayala remembers, José's wife and two children scoured the city in search of information about his fate. Márgara's anguish was more than justified: she soon found that he had been accused of treason against the Republic and imprisoned. Circumstances seemed to conspire against her: that same morning, the Valencian family in whose house they were living unceremoniously threw them out.

In spite of the housing shortage, they managed to find an apartment in a modern building with a lift. In order to get money with which to pay the exorbitant rent, Coco quickly got a job at the Foreign Press Office. Márgara, meanwhile, continued with her enquiries, which eventually led her to the Foreigners' Prison, where Pepe had been incarcerated. She visited him on two occasions before his final disappearance, and from both visits she returned with reassuring messages: it was all the result of a simple mistake, they had to let the investigation run its course, things would sort themselves out eventually. The prison was located beside the banks of the River Turia, and Márgara insisted that Miggie walk back and forth along one of the streets by the river, so her father could see her from the window of his cell.

It was a sad New Year for the Robles. Although the majority of their acquaintances expressed their incredulity and support over and over again, there were also some who turned their backs on them. Among these were two of Pepe's friends with the most influence at the time. One of them was Wenceslao Roces, then undersecretary of the Ministry of Education, and the other was Rafael Alberti. In a 1977 article, the surrealist writer and painter Eugenio Fernández Granell would reproach the poet Alberti for his silence about countless Stalinist murders, among them the death of 'Professor José Robles – poet and artist – ordered by the Russian Generals.' Only in a late book of conversations would Alberti mention the Robles case, but his statements were not especially revealing. According to Alberti, he and José Bergamín went to intercede on behalf of Robles before 'the authorities.' They told them of his relationship with Dos Passos and of the importance of the latter as a writer and as a fighter for liberty, 'but there was no way: they said it was proven that José Robles was a spy and they shot him.'

We have more proof of the steps taken on the other side of the Atlantic to liberate Robles. At the beginning of the year, Henry Carrington Lancaster requested the help of the US State Department, which replied that 'since Professor Robles is a Spanish subject there is nothing we here can do toward effecting his release.' At that time, however, the possibility that he might be executed still seemed unthinkable, and the family, deprived of their principal source of income, was preoccupied with simple subsistence, for which they appealed again to Lancaster to help them obtain financial aid. The Press Office was then under the auspices of the Ministry of Propaganda, installed in what had been the central building of the *Monte de Piedad* savings bank. At the end of January a cheque for three hundred dollars was received there, made out to Margarita Robles Villegas, Miggie being the only member of the family who had American citizenship.

In one of the letters addressed to his father's colleagues at Johns Hopkins Coco wrote: 'Nobody, from the Minister of State and the Russian Embassy down, has been able to find out a concrete reason for this ridiculous arrest.' The family's disquiet grew, however, as time passed, and by the time that cheque arrived they were seriously alarmed. José Robles was no longer in the Foreigners' Prison. He had told Márgara himself on her second visit to the prison that he was to be transferred to Madrid, but his whereabouts remained secret. What guarantees could they expect in a situation like that? Rumours began to circulate in Valencia about Robles' disappearance. Some suggested the possibility that he might have been taken to Russia or sent to the front; others spoke openly of his murder.

On 11 February, Maurice Coindreau wrote to Lancaster to inform him that he'd just received a letter from Márgara mentioning worries over her husband's life insurance policy, 'which of course is more important than ever for them,' indicating that her fears over Robles' fate had suddenly increased. Confirmation, still unofficial, of his death was given to Coco by Luis Rubio Hidalgo, his boss at the Press Office. It must have been one day at the end of February or the beginning of March, and that same evening Coco told his mother and sister in the lift on the way up to their flat.

# 2

When he arrived in Madrid at the end of October 1916, John Dos Passos was a young man who wanted to see the world and to write. This was his first contact with Spain and, although his stay was interrupted after three months, he had time to travel around much of the country. He usually dedicated Sundays to excursions to places near the capital: Aranjuez, El Pardo, the Sierra de Guadarrama and Toledo were some of his usual destinations. His friend José Giner, who accompanied him as a guide on several of these visits, in keeping with the ideals of the *Institución Libre de Enseñanza* where he'd been educated (he was the nephew of one of its founders), felt a sincere love for the towns and the lands of Spain. Later Dos Passos also went to La Mancha, whose landscape he'd so often glimpsed in the pages of *Don Quixote*, and crossed the eastern provinces from south to north up to Tarragona. He travelled in third-class carriages or simply on foot, and there was always someone who would pick him up in their cart or trap and share a bottle of wine. Dos' itineraries at that time are easy to reconstruct thanks to his letters and diaries, compiled by his biographer, Townsend Ludington. We can also gain a fuller insight into his impressions of the time from his own texts. 'I am mad about Spain,' he wrote in reference to the gentleness and nobility of its people. Dos Passos was indeed an enthusiast for Spain and all things Spanish. He loved the chocolate, the church bells, the long, gaily coloured scarves the people of Madrid wrapped round their faces on winter evenings, the custom of whiling away the time in cafés, even the constant commotion of the Puerta del Sol, 'the biggest & noisiest square in the city.' He also loved its history and culture, and soon had his room decorated with Velázquez and El Greco reproductions. For Dos Passos, Spain was a 'temple of anachronisms,' and in the Spanish way of dressing, in its music and rituals, in its pottery and gastronomy he perceived indications of a country that was at once Roman, Greek, Phoenician, Semitic and Arab. The poems he wrote then (and later collected in his only volume of poetry) celebrated the beauty and dignity of that eternal Spain, which he contrasted with the pragmatic materialism of more advanced countries. The disagreements he had with his friends from the *Institución Libre de Enseñanza*, supporters of the Europeanization of Spain, undoubtedly stemmed from this feeling.

He wouldn't return to Spain for another two and a half years. By then he was already a writer, though still unpublished. In fact, that August of 1919 he had come from London, where he'd just signed the contract for *One Man's Initiation: 1917*, a novel inspired by his experiences as an ambulance driver during the First World War. In the company of an American friend he travelled along the Cantabrian coast. From Motrico, in the province of Guipúzcoa, he wrote to Robles to announce his imminent arrival in the Spanish capital and to sing the praises of the

Basque Country coast: 'Everywhere there are dances, fireworks, fiestas, cider bars.' After climbing the Picos de Europa, he passed through Madrid on his way to Jaén, Málaga and Granada, where he settled for a while in mid-September. There he observed that, in the summer, the people of those places hire a fig-tree and go and live under it with their pigs and their goats and their cats and their chickens to eat the figs as they ripen and enjoy the shade: 'Life has no problems under those conditions.'

Dos continued to have an idyllic vision of Spain. Crossing the border meant for him leaving the 'fetid cloud' of Europe and at last breathing fresh air: 'The Bidasoa has become a Rubicon and the Pyrenees, thank God, are marvellously high.' His new position as the correspondent of a British Labour newspaper, *The Daily Herald*, took him to Lisbon for eight days in October. In Granada, he had to spend an entire month in bed suffering from a bout of rheumatic fever. He made use of this time to read and to work on what would be his first great literary success, the novel *Three Soldiers*. From the middle of November until the beginning of March of the following year he lived in Madrid. During those four months, as well as spending time with the friends he had in the city and visiting some of his favourite destinations (Aranjuez, Yepes, Toledo) with them, he tried to concentrate on writing his novel, which, like the previous one, recreated the horrors of the war he had witnessed. He wrote in the library of the Ateneo, for which José Giner had provided him with a pass. It was there that Pepe Robles introduced him to the man who would translate some of his books into French, Maurice Coindreau. Dos considered that library the most suitable place to work, and described it in a letter as 'abnormally full of literary-looking gentlemen, who busy themselves in heaps of books and make sad scholarly noises in their throats as they turn the pages.'

In March he travelled to Barcelona, and wrote to Robles from there to congratulate him on the birth of his son Coco and to inform him of his progress in the study of Catalan poetry: from what he'd read of him, Joan Maragall struck him as 'a great poet,' and in all the Catalan poets he perceived 'a pure and humble lyricism, with a scent of the earth that I like very much.' From Barcelona, after a brief stay in Palma in Mallorca, he would leave for France and then the United States in the middle of April.

Exactly a year later he was back in the Iberian Peninsula. On this occasion he was travelling with the poet E. E. Cummings, who was as anxious as he was to escape from New York literary life. They disembarked in Lisbon, and Dos Passos wrote to Pepe Robles announcing his intention to pass through Madrid and, in his unsteady Spanish, commented: 'It would be funny if I arrived in Madrid in time to see the premiere of sua comedia!' Robles never did premiere the play he was working on. Not long before, in 1920, he'd published in the Universal collection his translation of a drama by Alfred de Vigny: his eagerness to win over the theatre-going public went no further. In any case, his friend Dos could not have attended the improbable Madrid premiere either. Suffering from a painful toothache, Cummings was not in the ideal state to take an interest in local art and culture, as Dos had planned. He and Cummings left the Portuguese capital, and after brief visits to Salamanca and Plasencia, travelled to Seville, where a dentist finally lanced Cummings' abscess. The following days they devoted to attending bullfights and enjoying the sensuality of the Andalusian city, including that of its prostitutes, and then, apparently with no time to stop in Madrid, they left for France.

Dos Passos' adventures in Spain inspired, totally or partially, his next two books, both published in 1922. *Rosinante to the Road Again* clearly reflects the Spain that Dos wanted to find and did: a refuge to contrast with the materialist society of North America he'd so often criticized. His is a Spain of ancient virtues such as hospitality, attachment to the land and traditions, a Spain of poor men who nevertheless extend their hours of joy long into the night: the triumph of life and of human beings in a world of filth and rags. Combining metaphysics and realism, wavering between allegory and travel writing, combining the Spain of books with the Spain he experienced, Dos Passos proposed in *Rosinante to the Road Again* an interpretation of Spanish history and the Spanish character that was not far from the vision of the then prevailing generation of 1898. Not just the authors but also the preferred themes of that generation leap out from the pages of the book over and over again, and it's no accident that a certain immutable individualism, a trait that had previously defined the writers of '98, is also for Dos Passos the essence of Spain and all things Spanish. Based on the 'strong anarchistic reliance on the individual man,' he goes so far as to affirm that 'Spain is the classic home of the anarchist.'

In many of the poems in *A Pushcart at the Curb* he also

sings the praises of that individualistic, uncontaminated Spain. Of the six sections that make up the volume, two ('Winter in Castile' and 'Vagones de tercera,' of which Pepe Robles did a partial translation) are dedicated to Spain and illustrate Dos' wanderings: there are poems dedicated to Madrid, but also to Toledo, Aranjuez, Cercedilla, Navacerrada, Alcázar de San Juan, Getafe, Denia, Villajoyosa, Granada, Lanjarón... Professor Catalina Montes analyzed these compositions in 1980 and concluded that Dos Passos admired the dignity with which the Spanish accepted their economic backwardness: better to be poor than slaves 'to industrialization, to the yearning for money.'

His rejection of capitalism would deepen with the death sentences handed down to Sacco and Vanzetti, in whose innocence he believed absolutely. 'I was interested because the men were anarchists, and I had a good deal of sympathy

for their naive convictions,' he would write much later in *The Best Times*. Dos took their defence personally: he wrote a pamphlet denouncing the case, interviewed them and was a member of the committee set up to defend them. During the summer of 1927, in a renewed effort to prevent their execution, he published articles in several newspapers, and was arrested in Boston along with other demonstrators. The campaign had no effect whatsoever. Sacco and Vanzetti were executed on 23rd August, and Dos Passos, frustrated by the American capitalist system, which he considered guilty of the murder of the two anarchists, turned again towards socialism. In May of the following year he travelled to Russia to examine the new Soviet society. The resulting text, 'Russian Visa,' expressed his sympathies for the Russian people and their revolution, but also some reservations about the climate of fear and persecution that he perceived.

In February 1930, Dos Passos, this time with Katy on a pleasure trip, crossed Spain from north to south. In March they arrived in Cádiz, where they boarded the *Antonio López* for the Canary Islands and Cuba. His next trip, in the summer of 1933, would be more significant. By then, thanks to his participation in the Sacco and Vanzetti issue as well as his campaign denouncing the miners' labour conditions in Harlan County, Kentucky, he had become one of the most influential intellectuals of the left, and his intention was to write a long report on the young Spanish Republic, beacon of hope to so many. In fact, he'd just signed a contract for 'The Republic of Honest Men,' which would eventually appear, in April of the following year, published along with 'Russian Visa' and other journeys in the volume *In All Countries*. In a letter to Hemingway, he joked that his reportage project would be 'burned by Hitler, pissed on in the Kremlin, used for toilet paper by the anarchist syndicalists, deplored by *The Nation*, branded by *The New York Times*, derided by the *Daily Worker* and left unread by the Great American Public.'

Katy and Dos had planned to travel to Spain with Hemingway, who was going to scout film locations for a planned (though never made) adaptation of his book about bullfighting, *Death in the Afternoon*. However, another of Dos' attacks of rheumatic fever altered their plans. Katy and he arrived in July, and the first thing they did was to buy a little second-hand Fiat, which they called *Cockroach* and in which they'd cross the peninsula from south to north. In Pontevedra they witnessed a pyrotechnic display in which the fireworks burst out in the colours of the Republican flag, and in Santander they attended a meeting held by the socialist deputy Fernando de los Ríos, a cousin of José Giner. The event took place in the bullring, and someone released two doves meant to symbolize peace but, undoubtedly dizzy from the heat, they didn't manage to take off. Dos saw in this detail a bad omen for the fragile Republic, and perhaps an indication that the good times were ending for him too. In fact, more than thirty years later, when he wrote his memoirs, they concluded with this trip to Spain. Edmund Wilson couldn't help but offer a friendly reproach, and Townsend Ludington, alluding to the title of the book, *The Best Times*, would point out that the brief life of the Spanish Republic marked 'the last moments of the best times' for the writer.

In August, Katy and Dos settled in at the Hotel Alfonso in Madrid, which until 1931 had been called Alfonso XII. Hemingway arrived a few days later and took a room in the

Biarritz, but, too busy with his own affairs, only occasionally joined them for lunch at the Casa Botín. On his trips to Spain, Dos Passos had met several of the most outstanding intellectuals of the day: on his first visit he was received by Juan Ramón Jiménez, whose familiarity with American poetry astonished him, and on the second, he and Robles went to Segovia to visit Antonio Machado, whose work he intended to translate into English. On this trip he interviewed Manuel Azaña and Miguel de Unamuno. From both interviews Dos Passos emerged again sensing bad portents for the Republican regime. While waiting to be received by the president of the government, he felt 'the choking in my chest that comes from the breathed out air of government bureaus, the feeling of being cut off from the real world where men and women worked and suffered and enjoyed themselves.' When he saw Unamuno ('with his parchment skin and his narrow domed forehead he was getting to look more like Don Quijote than ever as the years went on'), the only comment on the Republic he could get out of him was: 'Where are the great men?'

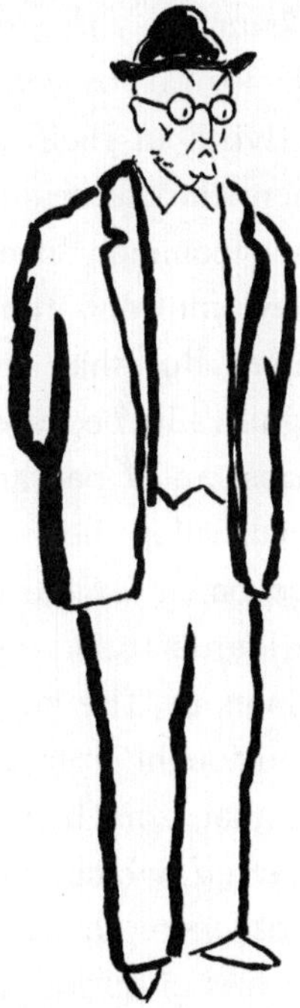

Ever loyal, Dos Passos also visited his Spanish friends. Pepe Giner showed him the Royal Palace (now called the National Palace), of which he'd been named curator, and what most caught Dos' attention was that, while Giner was making an inventory of the royal assets, he'd found the crown of Spain 'in a green baize bag stuffed into an old clothes closet.' He saw the other Pepe, Robles Pazos, who was in Madrid on vacation, especially at the *tertulias* in the cafés. It must have been in La Granja del Henar where José Robles introduced him to Ramón J. Sender, who had just returned from a trip to the USSR. The friendship between Sender and Dos Passos would resume quite a few years later in North America, and the Aragonese writer would recall it in his 1982 book *Álbum de radiografías secretas*. Their biographical and ideological trajectories followed parallel paths: left-wing activists in their youth, the Spanish Civil War converted them into ferocious anti-Communists, and only thanks to their common 'irrepressible independent judgement' could they confront the 'systematic defamation' that awaited them. But that encounter in the summer of 1933 was significant, because a few months before there had been a massacre of peasants by assault guards in Casas Viejas, a small village near Cadiz. This episode was more than just a bad omen for the new Republican regime; in fact it was a serious setback for its credibility. Sender, as Dos Passos relates in 'The Republic of Honest Men,' was the only one who fought from the pages of a newspaper to prevent the scandal from being covered up. Sender's chronicles in *La Libertad*, which would soon be collected and published as a book, were actually one of the American writer's principal sources of information.

Azaña's government, which initially denied the facts, eventually had to agree to an official investigation when the press revealed what had happened. For Sender, the later parliamentary skirmish was nothing but 'a fight between executioners, where they tried to discuss whether the executions had been carried out correctly or not.' For Dos Passos, the spirit of Casas Viejas would finally provoke the defeat of the government of honest men, and in his essay he condemned the powerlessness with which well-intentioned democrats contemplated 'the collapse of the very civilized life they prize so highly.' His old sympathies towards that genuinely Spanish individualism and anarchism fed a visceral mistrust of the politicians who had allowed them to be crushed.

His shattered confidence in the Republic went along with an aversion to the nascent bureaucracy. He and Katy suffered it firsthand at the end of September, when, about to leave Spain, they put their car up for sale. A young officer asked for permission to take it for a test drive and disappeared. The police quickly recovered *Cockroach*, and Dos went to the Puerta del Sol and saw the little Fiat swathed in chicken wire in the courtyard of *Gobernación*. There it was and there, retained as evidence, it would still be when Dos Passos and his wife set sail on the *Exochorda* from the port of Gibraltar. '*No hay remedio. Es la ley*,' the chief inspector told them, no matter how much they insisted on their urgent need to sell it. The episode with *Cockroach*, along with aftereffects of the illness still affecting Dos Passos, meant that their stay in Spain was also a failure on a personal level.

This, however, did not prevent his interest in the unstable state of contemporary Spain from remaining firm, and the old campaigner went back into action when a friend of his, the artist Luis Quintanilla, from Santander, was arrested in connection with the Asturian insurrection of October 1934 for forming part of the revolutionary committee in Madrid. Quintanilla was also (and especially) a friend of Hemingway's, with whom he'd got very drunk in a bar in Montparnasse in 1922. A man with an eventful life who in youth had been a sailor and a boxer and who had been a member of the Spanish Socialist Workers' Party (PSOE) since 1927 was going to be tried by a military court, and the sentence threatened to be particularly severe: the prosecutor was demanding sixteen years in prison.

To publicize the case and force the Spanish government to be lenient, Hemingway and Dos Passos organized an exhibition of Quintanilla's watercolours in the Pierre Matisse gallery in New York and, just as they were doing in England and France (at the initiative of André Malraux), promoted a campaign to collect signatures from personalities like Henri Matisse, Thomas Mann, Sinclair Lewis and Theodor Dreiser, with whom Dos Passos had collaborated in the defence of Sacco and Vanzetti. The exhibition was also to raise funds for the prisoners, and the two writers made use of their contacts among high society liberals. Among them were, for example, the wealthy and elegant Sara and Gerald Murphy, good friends of Hemingway and Dos Passos since the beginning of the previous decade. In her biography of the Murphys, Amanda Vaill reproduces a telegram from Gerald alluding to the exhibition's excellent reception: 'FOUR SOLD FIRST DAY.'

The catalogue included texts by both Hemingway and Dos Passos. Dos pointed out that 'Quintanilla has expressed his disgust in etchings and as an active revolutionist. It is natural that the civil and religious bureaucrats, the landlords and industrial exploiters who have used the army, the politicians-on-the-make and particularly those faithful watchdogs of property, the Civil Guards, to get back power in Spain for property, should have put him in jail.' The two novelists were not satisfied with merely helping their friend, but also sought to denounce the way the government had crushed the rebellion. 'It's not so very pretty to use Moorish troops, bombing planes and heavy artillery on your own people and towns,' wrote Dos Passos to Malcolm Cowley, director of *The New Republic*. One of his letters to Robles at the time reveals, nevertheless, the scepticism that such campaigns inspired. Although he's signed 'several of Barbusse's protests,' he says, and 'a petition in Quintanilla's case,' he didn't think that could influence Gil

Robles or Lerroux, who he calls in another letter 'that son of a bitch.'

To his surprise, things came out better than expected. In February 1935, Dos informed Edmund Wilson that Quintanilla had been moved 'into the fancy cell Juan March had fixed for himself and the rumor is that they'll let him off with six months.' At the end of May Quintanilla was already out on provisional liberty, and wrote a long letter to the novelist informing him of his new situation and expressing his gratitude: 'You cannot imagine what it means to read as the winter evening falls, in a jail cell, where all is humiliation and violence, the prologue that you two wrote for the catalogue of my exhibition.' The prosecutor had reduced his request to four years in prison, and it was unlikely that Quintanilla would have to return to jail.

Dos Passos' anxiety for the painter would revive in the summer of the following year, when reports arrived in the United States that he'd been murdered by fascist gunmen. Later it emerged that Quintanilla, who had participated in the assault on the Montaña Barracks in Madrid, was still alive. The Spanish Civil War had just broken out.

# 3

Dos Passos' preoccupation with the fate of the Spanish Republic led him, in the autumn of 1936, to propose the creation of a news service that would inform people of what was going on in an independent and truthful way. Dos thought that, by presenting Americans with accurate reports on the Spanish situation, the Roosevelt administration would be forced to allow the sale of arms to the government. By then quite a few people considered Dos Passos a Trotskyist, since his name was listed among the members of the American Committee for the Defense of Trotsky. In her biography of the writer, Virginia Spencer Carr has demonstrated that this inclusion occurred without his consent, but Dos Passos' commitment to causes of the left remained firm. Once he realized the news service project would not get off the ground, the novelist came up with the idea of filming a documentary showing the Spanish people's precarious living conditions during the war. He and Lillian Hellman, Archibald MacLeish and Ernest Hemingway formed a venture called Contemporary Historians, which would produce the film. They spoke to the Dutch director Joris Ivens, who was in the United States at the invitation of the New York Film Alliance and had begun work on a project for the Rockefeller Foundation. The cinematographer would be John Ferno, who often worked with Ivens.

Ivens and Ferno were both Communists. In *The Theme Is Freedom*, Dos Passos relates that shortly before embarking with Katy on the transatlantic steamer that would take them to Europe, he had dinner in New York with the anarchist Carlo Tresca, who warned him: 'John, they goin' make a monkey outa you... a beeg monkey.' When Dos replied that he and Hemingway had control over what was to be filmed, Tresca burst out laughing and reminded Dos that Ivens was a member of the Communist Party. According to him, everything they saw or did would be used by the party for its own interests. 'If the Communists don't like a man in Spain right away they shoot him,' he added.

Tresca's warnings did not alter the plans. Ivens would be in charge of production, and Hemingway, assisted by Dos Passos, of the script. Differences soon began to arise between the two old friends: while Dos wanted *The Spanish Earth* to centre on people's daily problems, Hem was interested in reflecting the progress of the military campaign. As Townsend Ludington suggests, such discrepancies might have masked others of a very different nature: Hemingway had just started a relationship with Martha Gellhorn, and his feelings of guilt towards his wife, Pauline, were probably intensified by the presence of Dos Passos and Katy, two of her best friends.

In spite of the fact that, unlike on previous occasions, Dos was not going to Spain to write articles or reportage but to collaborate on a propaganda film for the Republican cause, a good part of the journey can be reconstructed mostly thanks to the texts he wrote during those weeks for the media and which he would compile the following year in *Journeys Between Wars* as well as, although with reasonable reservations, to the novelistic recreation near the end of his life in *Century's Ebb*. He and Katy stopped first in Paris, where Dos found that French society was divided between the conservatives fearful of socialism and the leftists fearful of fascism. At a funeral for some young men killed by members of the organization of fascist sympathizers, Croix de Feu, led by Colonel Casimir de la Rocque, he spoke to ultra-rightwingers who accused the members of the Popular Front government of being lackeys of Moscow. He also went to the Quai de Bourbon to interview Léon Blum: 'He's a clear clever talker, is always ahead of you with some other lead when your lips start to form the word Spain.' The question of military aid to the Republic could not, therefore, be broached.

Following one piece of Carlo Tresca's advice, Katy did not accompany her husband to Spain. At the beginning of April, Dos said goodbye to her and took a train to Perpignan. In the café in the ancient stock exchange he found groups of men in dusty berets speaking in Catalan, and noted: 'More Spaniards, a considerable ragged refugee population that obviously didn't belong to the town.' He went to the Café Continental and asked for the owner, who introduced him to an individual who took him into a back room. On the wall was a map of Spain with the lines of the fronts marked with little flags. 'Ours,' said the man, indicating the Republican zone. Dos left the Continental to climb into the truck that was supposed to take him to Valencia. His driver was a French Communist who had worked as an upholsterer until he lost two fingers in an accident at work. The truck was carrying a cargo of machinery and field telephones and, to get them into Spanish territory, they had to pass through a couple of police checkpoints.

Once across the border, they made frequent stops to find the people responsible for providing them with fuel vouchers. In Gerona, Dos noted that 'the walls everywhere had been plastered with warposters' and 'the shopwindows were covered with thin strips of paper tape to keep them from breaking from the concussion of airplane bombs.' After spending the night in a hotel run by the anarchist union, the CNT, they left for Barcelona. The first thing they did was to go for a coffee on the Ramblas, where many of the premises exhibited signs announcing they were under 'Employee Control' or had been taken over by the CNT or the *Generalitat*. Then they drove around and around before finding a school transformed into the central warehouse for machine parts: that was where they had to leave their 'diemaking machinery.' They resumed their journey, and on their way through Sitges stopped at a bar belonging to one of the driver's friends, who 'was strong for the Valencia government and against Barcelona and all the local committees and tradeunions.' On the way to Tarragona, 'in the glare of our headlights on the whitewashed walls,' they saw five young men crossing the road in front of the truck. 'There was something curious about their walk. They were hopping on crutches. Each of them had lost a leg,' wrote Dos Passos. Later they picked up a hitchhiking militiaman who was going home on leave. They heard there had been bombings in Tortosa. 'Fine,' said the militiaman, thinking the town would be deserted, 'we'll go on to Tortosa and sleep quietly.' That was, in effect, what they did, and the next morning they bid the militiaman farewell in Castellón.

When they got to Valencia, Dos observed that the city did not look very different from the other times he had been there: 'The streets were crowded with miscellaneous-looking people and peddlers and signs almost like at the time of the annual fair, the only difference was the sprinkling of assorted military uniforms and the rifles and the pistol holsters and the tasseled militiamen's caps. Instead of bullfights the posters announced civil war.' In contrast to 'heroic Madrid' they talked of the 'festive Levante,' and Dos Passos' impressions coincide broadly speaking with those of Salazar Chapela, who wrote that 'we only knew there was a war on from the profusion of men in leather jackets, the construction of public shelters here and there, sandbags placed protectively in front of some doors and windows and the passing of the occasional truck, almost always at ninety kilometres an hour, carrying bearded and armed militiamen.'

Dos Passos and the driver stopped in front of the Hotel Internacional, next to the station and occupied for the most part by members of the International Brigades. There the novelist said goodbye to his travel companion, who had to deliver the truck and return to Paris by train. Immediately afterwards, he went to the foreign press office to present his credentials.

The Department of Press and Propaganda had its headquarters on the top floor of an old, dilapidated mansion, in the words of Arturo Barea, at the top of a 'shabby, sumptuous' staircase, across a reception room 'with faded red brocade on the walls,' through a labyrinth of corridors and small rooms 'overflowing with typewriters, roneos, rubber stamps, and packets of paper.' Constancia de la Mora, then deputy director and soon director of the Department, gives a quite similar description in her memoir, *In Place of Splendour*: 'floors littered with papers, walls grim with peeling paint, old tables and chairs covered with torn posters, carbon paper, copies of Polish, Swiss, German, British, and French newspapers.' In the middle of this chaos, the employees were preparing parcels, correcting articles and looking up addresses in the files, while the foreign correspondents waited in an adjoining room, sitting on a high-backed sofa that matched the two overstuffed armchairs in the room.

Dos Passos thought the office 'cosy and a little embarrassing, like a club. You meet old friends, you read the mimeographed sheets telling you what the government wants you to know. You snap at rumors. Inside, beyond a roomful of typewriters, the censor himself sits owllike in his big glasses at a little desk under a blue light.' From Dos Passos' description of him we know that the person who received him was the director of the Department, Luis Rubio Hidalgo, who features in both Barea's and Constancia de la Mora's autobiographical books. If Arturo Barea's portrait of Rubio Hidalgo is less than attractive ('the head, a pallid, hairless dome, and smoked glasses in tortoiseshell rims'), Constancia de la Mora's doesn't do much to improve his image: 'partly bald, with a tiny moustache, pasty-coloured face, and dark glasses,' whose unhealthy colour revealed the almost constant darkness of the office in which he worked.

This is not the first time the name of Luis Rubio Hidalgo

appears in this story: it had been he who, a month earlier, had unofficially given Coco Robles the news of his father's more than probable execution. That morning in April, a heartbroken Coco Robles came out to meet Dos in the Press Office and rapidly brought him up to date with events. The American writer's consternation is easy to imagine: the last news he'd had of his Spanish friend ('I knew that with his knowledge and taste he would be the most useful man in Spain for the purposes of our documentary film') was before his disappearance. His consternation, however, was tinged with incredulity. And also hope: if Pepe Robles' death had not been confirmed officially, it was still possible to consider it one of the many rumours that were picked up in places like that. Dos Passos emerged from his interview with Rubio Hidalgo with the promise that, the following day, in the course of a lunch with journalists, he could discuss the matter personally with the minister, Álvarez del Vayo.

That same afternoon he went to visit Márgara. The Robles family was no longer living in the building in Valencia where Coco had given his mother and sister the tragic news in the lift. A couple of weeks earlier, for financial reasons, they had moved to a modest flat nearby. Dos managed to find it without difficulty, and Márgara's desperate appearance and the precariousness of their living conditions convinced him of the gravity of the situation. Later he would comment to Maurice Coindreau that she had seemed 'actually very ill, with probably tuberculosis of one lung.' For Márgara, Dos Passos' unexpected appearance was one last hope to cling to. Considering who he was, the authorities would have to provide him with all the information she had been denied time and time again: why had her husband been arrested, what charges had been brought against him, whether or not it was true that he had been executed. It is not difficult to imagine the conversation between the two of them, and Dos Passos himself offers a few clues in *Century's Ebb*, in which José, Márgara, Coco and Miggie Robles appear respectively as Ramón, Amparo, Paco and Lou Echevarría. 'Could he have made enemies? He was pretty freespoken,' the writer's alter ego, Jay Pignatelli, asks Amparo, and she answers: 'Not recently. You wouldn't have known him. He became quite careful how he talked.'

Without giving names and including, perhaps deliberately, some slight imprecision, Dos Passos wrote about the tragedy of the Robles family in *Journeys Between Wars,* where he describes a 'woman with her children barely able to pay for the cheap airless apartment while she waits for her husband. It's nothing they have told her, he was just taken away for questioning, certain little matters to be cleared up, wartime, no need for alarm. But the days have gone by, months, no news. The standing in line at the police-station, the calling up of influential friends, the slowgrowing terror tearing the woman to pieces.' A little further on, he gives free rein to his worst fears over Pepe Robles' fate and speaks of 'the hundred ways a man may be guilty, the remark you dropped in a café that somebody wrote down, the letter you wrote last year, the sentence you scribbled on a scratchpad, the fact that your cousin is in the ranks of the enemy, and the strange sound your own words make in your ears when they are quoted in the indictment.' He goes on: 'They shove a cigarette in your hand and you walk out into the courtyard to face six men you have never seen before. They take aim. They wait for the order. They fire.'

Dos Passos was staying in the Casa de la Cultura, a hotel (The Palace) where the government had put up some Republican college professors and literary people who had lost their homes and was popularly known as the Casa de los Sabios or The House of the Wise. The novelist's state of mind prevented him from having fond memories of the place: 'It's dreary in the parlor there, dinner is a gloomy function there. It's like being in quarantine. We feel like old trunks in somebody's attic.'

The next day he attended the lunch Álvarez del Vayo threw for the foreign journalists at the Grao, 'the big old restaurant on the beach where years ago... the rice was just as good.' Dos Passos noted the 'curious whistling diction,' a result of his protruding lower jaw, in which the minister delivered his 'excellent' speech in Spanish and French, and left proof of his unease when he wrote: 'The wine is good. It's the old famous *paella* and the shrimps and the little clams. But the food at official luncheons does not digest.' Dos Passos had met Álvarez del Vayo in the Ateneo when he was a prestigious left-wing journalist, but he'd never struck him as particularly likeable. He managed to approach him at the end of the meal, and the minister insisted on talking about *The Spanish Earth*, and how he was prepared to offer the film crew all sorts of facilities. But what Dos Passos wanted to talk to him about was Robles. Álvarez del Vayo let him talk for a few moments, then claimed 'ignorance and chagrin,' promised to find out more about it and said a hasty goodbye. The writer watched him leave, surrounded by his retinue.

Ignorance about the Robles case, which had been one of the invariable topics of conversation among the displaced intellectuals in Valencia? Ignorance, when it's more than probable that Márgara had gone to him to ask for help? Dos Passos' allusion to the difficulty in digesting the paella could mask not only a sensation of unease but also a reasonable scepticism at the good wishes expressed by the minister. Would he fulfil his promise to find out more? Whatever the case, Dos Passos decided to continue his own investigations in Madrid.

It was that afternoon that he gave a statement to the correspondent from *Última Hora* that would appear in print on the 19th April under the headline 'The Spanish will destroy fascism in Europe and, consequently, in the world.' In the interview he spoke of his trip to Spain ('I found it very pleasant this time not to see the tricorns of the civil guards, which were very picturesque but too sinister') and the sympathies for the Republican cause demonstrated by artists such as Charlie Chaplin, Clark Gable and James Cagney. Later Dos Passos went for a walk by the port with some French journalists and saw some of the ships transporting arms for the Republic, 'the freighters with their names painted out that run without lights slipping through the blockades, the Mexicans as they are called; some of them are Russian but they can't all be Russian.'

Later he runs into 'an old friend who takes me to see the

place where the paintings from the Prado are stored.' Who was this old friend whose name Dos Passos leaves out? All indications lead to the conclusion that it was Luis Quintanilla, the artist from Santander whose release from prison Hemingway and Dos Passos had campaigned for after the failed insurrection in Asturias. In April 1937, Quintanilla was a member of the Junta for Seizure and Protection of Artistic Treasures, created by the Republican government with the aim of keeping the principal works of the national artistic heritage safe: that explains his ease of access to the vaults where the paintings from the Prado museum were stored. But in April 1937 Quintanilla was also a spy. Owing to his close friendship with Luis Araquistáin, the Republic's Ambassador to Paris, for several months Quintanilla had been gathering information among the groups of Spanish refugees in the south of France (principally in Biarritz and Bayona) and passing it on to the government through a network of contacts including the filmmaker Luis Buñuel. He visited Valencia frequently. He was there when Dos Passos arrived in the city and, although Dos describes the encounter as taking place later that day, the possibility cannot be ruled out that it might have happened during the lunch with Álvarez del Vayo, an old friend of Quintanilla's. What did the painter and the novelist talk about while they walked among the paintings and tapestries protected by double cement vaults? Undoubtedly, about Robles, and Quintanilla recommended the anguished Dos Passos should speak to his brother Pepe when he went to Madrid. Pepe Quintanilla, who appears in *Century's Ebb* as Juanito Posada, worked in the Republican counterespionage services as a member of the Police Brigade of the Socialist Group of Madrid (and, from August, of the *Servicio de Investigación Militar*, or SIM). Undoubtedly, Pepe Quintanilla would be able to help him find out what had happened to Robles.

After his encounter with the painter, Dos Passos spent another night in the Casa de la Cultura, and in the morning went to the Hotel Victoria: 'That nest of newspaper correspondents, governmental agents, spies, munitions salesmen and mystery women is empty and quiet now.' In front of the hotel the big Hispano-Suiza car that the *Generalitat* had put at the disposal of an unidentified 'famous French journalist' was waiting. The road to Madrid was in a much better condition than Dos Passos had expected it to be, and the travellers took advantage of stops at the various checkpoints to get out and stretch their legs. They didn't see any military traffic until they got to the outskirts of Alcalá de Henares: 'troops, field kitchens, youngsters in illfitting tin hats, [...] many trucks and men marching in formation.' The car dropped them off at the Hotel Florida, on the Plaza de Callao. There Dos Passos sensed the proximity of the front for the first time: 'While we are piling our bags on the pavement we stop suddenly. The noise that went on when the motor stopped was machineguns.'

The Florida was the hotel where foreign correspondents and writers were lodged, among them Hemingway, who was going around in a peculiar khaki uniform and a pair of shiny knee-high boots. The first person he knew that Dos Passos saw in the hotel was Sidney Franklin, a bullfighter from Brooklyn and good friend of Hemingway's, who had travelled from Valencia with Martha Gellhorn. The meeting between the two writers was curt. Hemingway asked how much food he'd brought and reacted indignantly when he saw Dos take out some bars of chocolate and four oranges: 'We damn near killed him.' The tension that had first been in evidence in New York persisted, and Hemingway's exaltation at the experience of the war, so far from Dos Passos' pacifist sensibility, was not likely to help matters.

Dos Passos wasted no time in resuming his investigation into what had happened to Robles. Of course, one of the people he went to speak to was Pepe Quintanilla, who, according to *Century's Ebb*, had his office in the Telefónica building on Gran Vía in Madrid. Pepe's nephew, Luis' son, Paul Quintanilla, has written in a biography of his father: 'Yes, Pepe told him, he was familiar with the facts of the case, but that they didn't possess any importance, and that he, Dos Passos, shouldn't give it any thought or worry about it.' Dos Passos was not satisfied with this reply and carried on investigating, but all the people he spoke to just kept assuring him that his friend would receive a fair trial. No one, however, could give him precise information on his whereabouts, and Dos, who still held out hope that Robles was in prison and checked through list after list, suspected that a conspiracy of silence and lies was being woven around him. Some time later, he would remember that all his inquiries disgusted some of his associates on the documentary project: What was one man's life at a time like that? They mustn't let personal feelings run away with them... Among those people was Hemingway. The long friendship between the two writers was about to disintegrate.

Not very far from the Hotel Florida, the Telefónica skyscraper ('the proud New York baroque tower of Wall Street's International Tel and Tel, the symbol of the colonizing power of the dollar') had become an emblem of the city's defence. 'Five months of intermittent shellfire have done remarkably little damage,' wrote Dos Passos. In that building, as well as Pepe Quintanilla's office, was the Madrid headquarters of the press and censorship office, where the novelist met 'a cadaverous Spaniard and a plump little pleasantvoiced Austrian woman,' who were Arturo Barea and his companion, Ilsa Kulcsar. Barea, who had not yet published any books, had been contracted by Luis Rubio Hidalgo in the first weeks of the conflict. Later when his boss followed the Republican government to Valencia, Barea had to take charge of the Madrid office and the five employees who remained in the capital. Ilsa arrived in November 1936. A veteran socialist who had travelled to Spain to participate in the fight against fascism, she helped him to reorganize the foreign press and censorship service. The abandonment of the department had sparked off a struggle for its control. Proof of this is the fact that *Pravda*'s reporter, Mikhail Koltsov (a man of great authority in spite of Koestler's description of him as a 'short, thin, insignificant-looking man, with a quiet manner and pale eyes'), had shown up at the office and threatened Barea: 'This is a scandal. Whoever is responsible for this kind of sabotage deserves to be shot.' Between such tensions and a job that took up eighteen hours of every day, Barea's physical and mental health suffered gravely: it's not surprising that Dos Passos portrays him as 'a nervous man; he looks underslept and underfed.'

When he wrote this, he couldn't have known how pertinent his impressions were. The day before, a shell fragment had flown into Barea and Kulcsar's room in the Hotel Gran Vía and reduced all of Ilsa's shoes to 'a pitiful heap of scorched, twisted, tortured-looking leather.' Around the corner on Calle de la Montera, Barea had seen a still-twitching piece of human brain spattered on a shop window. That, combined with two bombings he'd witnessed from the hotel room window, provoked a nervous collapse that kept him practically incapacitated for several weeks. That afternoon in the Press Office, while Dos Passos was giving him a signed copy of *The 42nd Parallel*, Barea was on the verge of sinking into what would later be diagnosed as shell shock, which often includes fever and vomiting but also nightmares, hallucinations, panic attacks: 'People and things near me grew blurred and twisted into phantom shapes as soon as they were out of direct contact with me. I was afraid of being shut up and alone, and afraid of being in the open among people.' His pitiful state, however, did not prevent him from later recording in *The Forging of a Rebel* his and Ilsa's meeting with 'a guest whom I liked and respected, John Dos Passos, who spoke about our land workers and peasants with a gentle understanding, looking from one to the other out of wondering brown eyes.'

Strangely enough Barea's breakdown had been brewing while he and Ilsa attended a delegation of British ladies headed by the Duchess of Atholl, and Dos Passos was going to allude to these very same women in one of his pieces written during those days. Barea and Ilsa were in charge of organizing a few days of 'war tourism' for them which included an excursion through bombarded Madrid, a visit to the front, an official reception offered by General Miaja... When the manager of the hotel told them of the fire the shell fragment had caused in their room, the ladies went upstairs with them and sympathized with Ilsa over the loss of her shoes. The episode that Dos Passos wrote about also took place in the Hotel Gran Vía, specifically in the subterranean dining room where the correspondents gathered to eat their sad rations. At the tables there were militiamen and internationals on sprees and 'a sprinkling of young ladies of the between the sheets brigade,' and a drunk, seeing how well the duchess and the other ladies had dined, protested so angrily that the waiters eventually served the journalists 'a couple of long-dead whitings and a plate of spinach which they'd probably been planning to eat themselves.'

In *The Clash* Barea wrote: 'Drinks at the Gran Vía bar and drinks at Miami bar.' The foreign journalists and writers moved in 'a circle of their own and an atmosphere of their own, with a fringe of men from the International Brigades, Spaniards who touted for news and tarts.' That was also the atmosphere Dos Passos found during that stay in Madrid. His texts from that April included in *Journeys Between Wars* reflect his walks through the besieged city: the first defence barricade, very close to the hotel; the next barricade, where a smiling Cuban sentry asked to see his pass; the trenches made of sandbags in the Plaza de España, in one corner of which a group from the International Brigade waited to be fed... Later, 'you open a groundglass door and find... the front. The rest of the house has been blown away. The groundglass door opens on air, at your feet a well opens full of broken masonry and smashed furniture, then the empty avenue and beyond, across the Manzanares, a magnificent view of the enemy.' That was probably when one of the encounters with Hemingway alluded to in *Century's Ebb* occurred. According to Dos Passos, Hemingway had gone on a rash stroll at the front in the company of a British scientist. They were both within range of Franco's artillery and, when a Republican army corporal reproached them for their lack of caution, they just walked away haughtily. A short time later, Dos Passos met them 'puffed up like turkey gobblers.' If they hadn't been shot it was because it was lunchtime and, at least in theory, Spanish soldiers waited till they'd finished lunch before going back to shooting at each other.

On another of his walks Dos Passos couldn't help but notice that the Hotel Alfonso (where he'd stayed with Katy in the summer of 1933) had been hit by so many shells it looked like a Swiss cheese. And on another, he came upon 'the division El Campesino in new khaki uniforms parading with flags and Italian guns and trucks captured at Brihuega.'

He made few trips outside of Madrid. The one that stood out was the visit to the field headquarters of the International Brigade in the ancient castle of the Duke of Tovar, in the province of Guadalajara. Along with other correspondents, Dos Passos was invited to the ceremony celebrating the creation of a new brigade, formed out of the old Fifteenth Brigade. As well as several high-ranking Ministry of War officials, Generals Walter, Miaja, Líster, and Colonel Rojo were present. The troops were inspected, speeches were delivered in Spanish, French, German and

Russian, and finally the flamenco dancer Pastora Imperio and the singer Pastora Pavón ('La Niña de los Peines'), to whom Hemingway would pay homage in *For Whom the Bell Tolls*, performed for the soldiers assembled there. 'The way things are going the fiesta was heartbreaking, the cheers, the marching troops, the *Hymn of Riego*, the speeches by youthful commanders who had been carpenters or stevedores or blacksmiths in private life,' Dos Passos writes in *Century's Ebb*.

María Teresa León talks in her *Melancholy Memoir* of a photo taken at the front of her, Dos Passos, Alberti, Hemingway and General Walter, 'who was later killed just when he entered Warsaw victoriously after kissing the ground that was his own twice over.' That was the day the photo was taken. Alberti and María Teresa had returned

from Moscow not long before, and Dos Passos and Alberti had probably already seen each other in Madrid. What is certain is that, wherever this first encounter took place, the tragic fate of Robles Pazos had taken up a good deal of their conversation.

Before Dos Passos arrived in Spain, Rafael Alberti had already gone to 'the authorities' for the same reason. It seems, in any case, that their mutual sympathies were limited. Already in a letter from 1934 to Pepe Robles, Dos Passos had referred to the Andalusian with a certain disdain: 'Did I write to tell you I'd received Alberti's poetry? He's a nice lad, but frankly, don't his poems seem a little drab? If all the talentless lads become revolutionaries, we won't have a revolution till Judgement Day.' Now, with Alberti converted into one of the brightest stars of Spanish Communism, Dos Passos' old reticence must have been bolstered, and Márgara's complaints about the behaviour of some of her husband's old friends could not have been far from his mind; those who, having been in a position to help her, didn't even ask how she was. Which old friends were these complaints about? Those who had acquired fame and influence with the growing power of the Communist Party: one of these was the then undersecretary of the Ministry of Education, Wenceslao Roces; another, Alberti himself, who, while Dos Passos was on the point of discovering the tragic destiny fate had held in store for Robles, was being received at the Kremlin. The Communist press made much of that reception. The day after the Fifteenth Brigade fiesta, Dos Passos read Alberti's statements in the newspaper *Ahora*, the organ of JSU (*Juventudes Socialistas Unificadas*, in fact controlled by the Communists, rather than the Socialist Party): 'I have great faith – comrade Stalin told us – in the youth of Spain.' And four days later he might have also read the article that María Teresa León published in the same paper about the warm welcome she and her husband had been given at the Kremlin. Around the same time *Mundo Obrero* devoted half a page to them and Alberti praised Stalin as 'so nobly human,' 'so simply affectionate.'

The photo María Teresa León is talking about must be the last one of Dos Passos and Hemingway together, since their falling out happened that very afternoon. Among the other correspondents attending the military celebration was the writer Josephine Herbst, who in *The Starched Blue Sky of Spain* has left us the most complete version of what happened. Like the others, Josie Herbst was staying at the Hotel Florida, and Dos Passos mentions her indirectly in one of his Spanish chronicles, where he relates an early-morning shelling of the hotel. From the dispatches Hemingway sent during those days to the North American Newspaper Alliance (NANA) we can imagine the consequences of those bombardments, such as 'a heap of rubble, smashed cement and thrown up dirt, a single dead man, his torn clothes dusty, and a great hole in the sidewalk from which the gas from a broken main is rising, looking like a heat mirage in the cold morning air.' Dos Passos experienced the shelling from inside the hotel: 'Again the shriek, the roar, rattle, tinkle of a shell bursting somewhere. Then silence again, cut only by the thin yelps of a hurt dog, and very slowly from one of the roofs below, a smudge of dirty yellow smoke forms, rises, thickens and spreads out in the still air under the low indigo sky.' The shells kept coming and, in the midst of the confusion and the guests' hurried, semi-clad dashes, 'a completely dressed woman novelist from Iowa' took charge of the coffee and handed it around in glasses.

Josephine Herbst was born in Sioux City, Iowa, in 1892. On 17th April, after the shelling woke up the hotel guests in the middle of the night, Hemingway invited her for a cognac in his room on the fourth floor. Making use of Josie's long friendship with Dos Passos, he wanted her to speak to him and persuade him to stop trying to find out about Robles. But she already knew that Robles was dead: she'd been told confidentially in Valencia by someone who, concerned by Dos' investigative zeal, feared 'he might turn against their cause if he discovered the truth, and hoped to keep him from finding out anything about it while he was in Spain.' The problem was that Josie, to protect her informant's anonymity, had promised to keep it secret. Now, however, she thought it unfair to keep Dos in his 'anguished ignorance,' and told Hemingway the truth: 'The man is already dead. Quintanilla should have told Dos.' Hemingway was taken by surprise by the news. What could they do? Tell him, of course. But, since Josie had promised not to, Hemingway decided that he himself would tell him as soon as the opportunity presented itself and that he would allege to have heard from 'someone from Valencia who was passing through but whose name he must withhold.'

That was the day of the fiesta at the Fifteenth Brigade. Rafael Alberti and María Teresa León had been in charge of inviting the American writers. In spite of her admiration for Alberti's *Concerning the Angels*, Josephine Herbst could not help but feel displeased at the couple's presence, whose animated chatter, 'which went on with the vivacity of bright canaries, did not strike a sympathetic note in me,' and would have preferred to spare herself the poet's company, with his 'sparkling military boots and with his camera in hand, and his propensity for arranging groups for pictures, then leaping into the center of the group at the last moment while he thrust the camera into someone else's hand.' The lunch took place in a reception room decorated with portraits of the Duke of Tovar's ancestors. By the time the coffee was served, Hemingway had already spoken to Dos Passos, and he, with a cup in his hand, approached Josie Herbst and 'in an agitated voice asked why was it that he couldn't meet the man who had conveyed the news, why couldn't he speak to him too.' The only thing she could manage to tell him was to wait till he got to Valencia and try to find out more there through someone like Álvarez del Vayo.

The Albertis and the three American writers returned to Madrid in the same car. Except for the 'chirping' with which María Teresa tried to lessen the tension, the trip was made in complete silence. As soon as the car stopped in front of the hotel, Hemingway and the Albertis rushed away. Before going to their respective rooms, Herbst and Dos Passos went for a nocturnal stroll in the Plaza Mayor.

That, in summary, is Josephine Herbst's story. The interpretation Stephen Koch makes of it, in his book *Double Lives*, is quite different. Koch starts from the supposition that 'the Comintern agent' Herbst was 'sent to Spain to help monitor and control the American literary celebrities in Madrid.' According to Koch, Josephine Herbst, who had left Valencia after a briefing by her colleagues of the secret police *apparat*, 'arranged for the public humiliation and discredit of her dear friend John Dos Passos, while surreptitiously spreading the lie that his close friend in Spain was a fascist spy and had been shot for it.' With that aim, again according to Koch, she wove a plan, choosing a suitable time and place for the revelation ('a large public gathering of noteworthy Russians and Germans and other foreign VIPs'), as well as the ideal emissary, and 'she watched with knowing interest as it visibly aroused Hemingway's sadism.' It would all be a studied and effective staging, and the *apparat*, which 'had embarked upon a courtship of Hemingway while simultaneously undertaking to discredit the too-inquisitive Dos Passos,' must have congratulated Herbst effusively for having been able to create 'the very public impression that Hemingway was a politically reliable person while Dos Passos was not.'

A simple comparison of the versions of Herbst and Koch demonstrates the cheerful irresponsibility with which the latter has deformed the facts to adapt them to his prejudices and fantasies (or perhaps simply to his misinformation: he refers to Robles Pazos as Robles Villa throughout). The details with which he adorns the story speak for themselves. Note the way 'Hemingway swaggered up to Dos Passos in full view of the many people who were gathering round them in circles, and announced as cuttingly as possible' the news of Robles' death, while 'Herbst stood at a distance, anonymous and safe, watching her handiwork take its cruel effect.' As cuttingly as possible? Cruel effect? Koch's distortion of the original story never lets up, but his meticulous betrayal of any idea of objectivity is never so alarming as when he decides to give free rein to his inventiveness and slip in here and there as verified facts things that are no more than mere conjecture. Herbst and Hemingway, for example, had made a pact that the source of the news was supposedly a 'German correspondent,' and present at the Fifteenth Brigade fiesta was Otto Katz, one of the Communist propaganda chiefs Koch alludes to so frequently in his book, whose 'cover on this occasion, as it was on many other occasions, might very well have been that of "a German correspondent".' What proof does he offer that Katz, Josephine Herbst's 'mentor, guide and quite possibly control,' 'was almost certainly on the sidelines too, likewise watching'? Absolutely none, and in any case, even if it were true that Katz was at the fiesta, it wouldn't prove anything either: what would be odd in that, given that it was a celebration of the International Brigades?

Koch's version would have some basis if Josie Herbst had really been a Soviet agent. Unfortunately for Koch, she was not. Although he himself admits he had 'seen no evidence either to prove or refute that Josephine Herbst was an agent,' his conjectures (again the conjectures) are based on two facts. The first is that, apparently, the Communist *apparat* had at some point trusted Josie's husband, a little-known writer called John Herrmann, with some espionage mission. The second, that Herbst herself would be dismissed in 1942, for presumed Communist sympathies, from the US intelligence agency she had joined after the Japanese bombing of Pearl Harbor.

Both events are thoroughly examined in Elinor Langer's biography of Josephine Herbst published in the early 1980s. Nothing in this biography leads one to believe that

Herbst was what *Double Lives* states that she was, and here too it's difficult to overlook Koch's efforts to deform reality in such a way that it ends up justifying his peculiar witch hunt. As for Herrmann (from whom Josie had separated in 1932), Langer recounts that between 1934 and 1935, he took part in the 'transmission of materials between Party officials in Washington and Party officials in New York.' What materials were these? All evidence indicates that they were documents regarding official programmes of agricultural development that the American Communists hoped to use for their own political interests. That is all: the distinguished figure of Soviet espionage that Koch believes he has identified in Herrmann turns out to be nothing more than a simple Party snitch.

As for the second point, Elinor Langer's investigation is no less revealing. At the end of December 1941, Josephine Herbst began to work in the Office of the Coordinator of Information (OCI), an independent intelligence agency that, among other tasks, organized propaganda radio broadcasts to the countries with which the United States was at war. Josie, who spoke fluent German, formed part of the team of scriptwriters for the transmissions in that language and, in effect, the FBI began to investigate her to determine the nature of her relations with the Communist Party and with the USSR. The investigation would conclude with Herbst's official exoneration (a detail, incidentally, which Koch takes it upon himself to conceal), but by then the director of the OCI had already dispensed with her services. The FBI investigators collected numerous statements about Josie's political activities, and the most striking thing is that among the confidential informants who accused her was another well-known writer of the time. In May 1942, the fanciful Katherine Anne Porter travelled to Reno, Nevada, to get a divorce from her fourth husband, and while there, conveniently protected by anonymity, testified against Josephine, who had been her 'friend' and would continue to be for some years to come. In her book, Elinor Langer not only reveals the identity of the informant but also reproduces her declaration to the federal authorities, in order to examine what was true and what was false in her accusations, and dismantles the most compromising of them: that Josie had worked as a courier in the pay of the Soviet government.

Apparently, Katherine Anne Porter's fibs, which were not even believed by the FBI investigators, did seem credible to Stephen Koch, and the portrait he gives of Josephine Herbst is not only deranged but offensive. Not surprisingly, shortly after the publication of *Double Lives*, Elinor Langer herself hastened to refute his assertions in *The Nation*. As she states in her article 'The Secret Drawer,' Koch's book 'is an attack on the integrity of the entire generation of Western intellectuals that came of age in the period after the Russian Revolution.'

Langer's work demonstrates, furthermore, that Herbst's version of what happened on 17th April in the Duke of Tovar's former castle is reliable. That night, Josie and Dos went for a walk to the Plaza Mayor. Alone and sad in bombed-out old Madrid, they had more things in common than they might have imagined. What they'd seen and experienced during those days in Spain inevitably influenced both their later ideological development. We've already seen the first symptoms of Dos Passos' transformation. As for Herbst, we can simply quote Langer when she says that, upon her return from Spain, she 'ended her connections with the Communist Party. She had learned too much. Never having joined, she did not publicly resign nor did she take any other public actions, but she stopped seeing the people she had been associated with before; in her own mind she "broke"; and she was never politically active again.'

Two years later, Dos Passos would write to Herbst and, in reference to that early morning of shelling, tell her: 'I shall always remember how human you looked and acted at the old Florida that morning – amid many depressing circumstances that was one thing that made me feel good.' Among those circumstances was, of course, Robles' death, which Dos Passos had come to realize was true before Hemingway believed himself to be revealing it. If we go by the fictionalized version in *Century's Ebb*, it must have been Pepe Quintanilla who told him. 'The man has been shot,' Juanito Posada (Pepe Quintanilla) tells him while they drink whiskey, and then adds: 'I will see to it his wife and children are not molested... I promise... but from now on... silence.' And, in a letter to the editor of the *New Republic* in July 1939, Dos Passos wrote that he received definite information that Robles had been executed, from someone he calls 'the then chief of republican counterespionage service,' in Madrid (someone like Posada-Quintanilla).

So it seems probable that, before going to the fiesta at the Fifteenth Brigade, Dos Passos already knew what had happened, which means that his break with Hemingway was not to do with the fact that he had given him the tragic news. Their break had to do with the scant sensibility Hemingway showed towards human pain: that was war, what did the life of one man matter? In the words of Josephine Herbst, 'Dos hated war of all kinds and suffered in Madrid not only from the fate of his friend but from the attitude of certain people on the fringe of war who appeared to be taking it as a sport.' Could there be a clearer reference to Hemingway, for whom the war had provided the perfect occasion for exhibitionism and boastfulness?

Dos Passos left Madrid shortly after the fiesta at the Fifteenth Brigade. Although other statements contradict such accusations, Hemingway would later call his former friend's courage into question: 'The very first time his hotel was bombed, Dos packed up and hurried back to France.' Nevertheless, as Hemingway knew, Dos Passos' abrupt departure was not due to cowardice but to the consternation caused by everything he had discovered. In a letter of July 1939 he explained: 'After my American friends started to give tongue I decided that it was useless to stay longer in Spain and that my being there might be dangerous to the people I was associating with.'

Those who had kept quiet about the murder of Robles had done so for two reasons: in the first place, because they wanted to avoid its use as propaganda against the Republic; second, out of fear that confiding the truth to Dos Passos would have put them in danger. The American novelist had not managed to find out much about his Spanish friend, but his investigations had led him to glimpse one of the sources of that fear: the comprehensive extralegal police and prison system in the hands of the NKVD, the Soviet secret police.

After the first stages of the conflict, when the various left-wing organizations had set up provisional jails, the NKVD developed a network of prisons to discipline (or liquidate) members of the International Brigades. Using this as a pretext for a sort of extraterritoriality (and almost beyond control and any appearance of respect for legality), its creator had been the chief of the NKVD in Spain, Alexander Orlov. The network consisted not only of *chekas* and prisons but even had its own crematorium to get rid of the corpses; according to Stanley G. Payne, an increasing number of Spanish dissidents were incarcerated and executed in those locales along with citizens of other nationalities. Was the Foreigners' Prison where Márgara visited her husband on two occasions part of this sinister system? According to Miggie Robles, the prison was located beside the Turia riverbed. Also near the Turia, in the building that today houses the Museo Fallero, was the Monteolivete jail, which was turned into the Military Prison after the war. The possibility exists, therefore, that this prison for brigaders had been set up in one of the Monteolivete's buildings, but that doesn't change things: the sign, visible to Miggie and to all those who passed that way, supports the hypothesis of penitentiary extraterritoriality.

The final chronicle from Madrid in *Journeys Between Wars* recreates Dos Passos' departure from the city. As he passed the Cibeles fountain, two shells exploded somewhere up the Paseo de la Castellana. The car carried on towards the Puerta de Alcalá and went past 'the now closed café under the trees opposite the postoffice where the last time I was in Madrid I used to sit late in the summer evenings chatting

with friends, some of whom are only very recently dead.' The café was obviously La Granja del Henar, and the plural of 'friends' only half-concealed the allusion to Robles Pazos, with whom he had shared so many *tertulias* at the marble-topped tables of the Calle de Alcalá. With this coded reference, Dos Passos said farewell both to Madrid and to his dead friend.

So why was José Robles killed? Dos Passos kept asking himself the same question for a long time. In a letter to Henry Carrington Lancaster in early November he says it seemed 'certain that Robles was shot for some reason by the Communist GPU [NKVD], and nobody dares open their mouths about it. Why he was shot I still have hopes to find out.' A few months before, in July, Márgara had also written to Lancaster to tell him that 'a fatal mistake or perhaps personal vengeance' seemed to her the only possible explanations for her husband's death.

The final reasons will probably never be known, but we can dismantle some of the unfounded rumours that fed the accusations of treason against Robles. Among these was the help he had supposedly given to his brother Ramón to pass into the so-called national zone and join the rebel army. A simple glimpse at his brother's service record serves to refute such a claim. When the military rebellion occurred, Ramón Robles Pazos, two years younger than Pepe and a veteran of the Africa war, was employed as a captain in the infantry and was on vacation in Madrid. Evidence of his ideological orientation is offered by the fact that, on 21st July, just days after the uprising, he tried to get to Toledo to contribute to the defence of the Alcázar fortress, which would eventually carry such a symbolic charge for Franco's side. He didn't manage it. He was arrested in Getafe and taken to a *cheka* in Madrid, on the Paseo de las Delicias, which he left that same night. Did his older brother have something to do with this rapid release? It is possible. What does seem sure is that Pepe tried to convince him to offer his services to the Republic, so desperately in need of officers at that time.

Whatever commitment Ramón might have undertaken, he managed to remain unnoticed for almost three months in besieged Madrid, and on 16th October was again arrested, this time 'for not rendering service of any kind.' Transferred to the Buenavista police station, on Calle Hermosilla, he continued to refuse to 'serve in the ranks of the "Red" Army,' and four days later was imprisoned in the Model Prison, from which he emerged a month later to be transferred to the Ventas Prison. There he remained locked up until, on the 26th of the following January, after reiterating his refusal and being charged with disaffection, he was granted provisional freedom. The dates leave no room for dispute: by this time, it was more than two and a half months since Pepe Robles had left Madrid and approximately a month and a half since he'd disappeared from the flat in Valencia.

The escape, in fact, did not happen until much later. On 28th January, just two days after his release, Ramón sought refuge in the Chilean Embassy, where he coincided with the Falangist writer Rafael Sánchez Mazas. On 19th February, he managed to get moved to the French Embassy, where he remained for eleven months. On 18th January 1938, 'still under the protection of France,' several young men of military age were taken from the Embassy and driven by car to the Tembleque railway station, in the province of Toledo, where they set out for the coastal town of Caldetas, near Barcelona. Two months later, Ramón managed to embark on a French destroyer, anchored a mile out from the beach, and arrived at Port-Vendres, the first port on the other side of the border. Another two months would go by before, by way of Hendaye, he managed to get back into Spain on Franco's side. On 20th May he reported for duty in Burgos. On 21st June he was promoted to major and on the 26th went into combat in command of a platoon of *Regulares*. By then it was a year and four months since his brother Pepe had been murdered in Valencia.

There was another even more crude and ludicrous rumour going around. In June 1986, Stephen Koch interviewed an elderly Joris Ivens, who, still convinced that the accusations against Robles were true, told him that he had been 'using a concealed light to flash signals to the fascist lines.' Ivens' version needs no refuting, as it would be difficult for someone to communicate with the enemy by means of light signals at such a time, when the nearest front, as an enormous sign installed in the central Plaza de Castelar proclaimed, was one hundred and forty kilometres away from Valencia.

According to an anonymous document found in one of

the family's apartments by Cristina Allott, Robles' great-niece, his fall from grace resulted, according to 'his son's opinion,' from his being too frank and indiscreet in the *tertulias* and 'not having a political background and never having joined any political group.' This version matches that offered by Francisco Ayala, for whom, 'it was said, some careless comment he'd made during a *tertulia* in the café gave a hint of some otherwise anodyne news, which could only have been known from a cable in code, and that cost him his life.' Did Robles commit some such indiscretion? We cannot know. Nevertheless it is probable that his fate would have been the same whether he had done so or not. José Robles was a loyal Republican but he was not a Communist, and as an interpreter for the Soviet military advisors he had become a 'man who knew too much.'

Recently declassified confidential reports demonstrate that the Kremlin's plans, on the one hand, to control the War Ministry, and on the other, to crush the CNT and the POUM were documented from the very beginning of the Russian military collaboration with the Republic, and there is even a report from Gorev himself in which he says 'a struggle against the anarchists is absolutely inevitable.' Robles must have known about those plans. Robles knew too much about the growing Soviet power within the Spanish government and about the fierce repression that was looming, and that was enough to make him suspect in the eyes of Soviet military intelligence, because, as a non-Communist, he would not be sufficiently trusted to 'forget' the information acquired from Miaja and Gorev.

It is probable that Robles was murdered not because he

would have talked but so that he couldn't talk, and for Dos Passos, who never credited the thesis of the supposed indiscretion, his death had the desired effect of making people very cautious when they spoke of the Russians. It was therefore a warning: those who didn't want to meet the same fate as Robles had to keep quiet about all that they saw and didn't like, had to join that immense conspiracy of silence that Dos himself had run up against while investigating what had happened to his friend.

# 4

In order for a murder to have been committed there must be a murderer, and at some point in this story the question of who killed Robles would have to arise. If documentation about the case exists in the NKVD archives, deposited in the Central Archive of the Federal Security Services in Moscow, surely the names of the perpetrator and his collaborators must figure. That would, undoubtedly, be the most direct route to untangling the enigma, but it did not appear simple. Daniel Kowalsky, in *Stalin and the Spanish Civil War,* declares that this archive 'continues to maintain impenetrable levels of secrecy': his one and only visit 'was greeted with contemptuous laughter and conclusive rejection.' I requested advice from specialists, on the off chance that they would be able to help me, but their replies did not encourage optimism. Stanley Payne informed me that those archives were 'totally closed to foreigners (and to almost all Russians)' and that, while a few years ago some researchers managed to consult them, at the present time 'the window had closed.' Having this route ruled out, what could I do? Wait for an improbable opening of the window before finishing my investigations? Publish provisional conclusions and trust that someone would complete them in the future? In the most unexpected way, while I tried to resolve the dilemma, a new route, albeit an indirect one, opened up before me.

At the beginning of November 2003, the writer Andrés Trapiello told me about an exhibition of paintings by a friend of his, Carlos García-Alix, that he knew would interest me. It was called *Madrid-Moscow* and was showing in a gallery on Calle del Barquillo until the middle of December. I was planning to spend a few days in Madrid looking things up in the Municipal Newspaper and Periodicals Library, and the first thing I did when I arrived was visit the art gallery. The paintings were of exceptional quality, superb recreations of atmospheres and revealing an evident fascination for rationalist architecture, but what most caught my attention was the rare familiarity the painter had with the cityscapes the Soviet envoys had frequented. In one of the paintings was the façade of Gaylord's Hotel, which had been one of their principal centres of operations. In another is the Cine Europa, the cellar of which had housed a *cheka*. In a third I recognized

Mikhail Koltsov among the mysterious figures portrayed in front of the Bar María Cristina.

I called Andrés Trapiello to pass on my impressions, and we arranged to have dinner together the next day. I arrived at the appointed place, and Andrés introduced me to the person on his left. It was Carlos García-Alix. Of course, the conversation immediately turned to the activities of the Soviet agents during the war. The familiarity I'd sensed from the paintings was, in reality, far greater than anyone could have imagined. The names of Gorev, Berzin or Koltsov, along with others I had never heard mentioned, were invoked by Carlos as naturally as someone referring to recently deceased close friends or relatives. When I asked him about his sources of information, he admitted that he had read books on the subject in several languages and had even had some Russian works translated for his personal use. At some point, he asked me: 'Do you want to know who killed Robles?' Noticing how taken aback I was, he clarified: 'I can't assure you he was the one who killed him. But I can assure you he was directly related to his death. It is simpler than it seems. You just have to know who Orlov's man in Valencia was at that time. Do you want to know who it was?' Then and there, he slowly pronounced a name and a surname, and pointed me towards the first in a series of clues I had to follow to arrive on my own at the same conclusion. That clue was a book and it was called *Nosotros, los asesinos*.

The author of *We, the Murderers*, the journalist Eduardo de Guzmán, could have appeared in this story as one of those soon-forgotten, minor characters. Although Dos Passos, in

'The Republic of Honest Men,' stated that Ramón J. Sender had been the only one who had raised his voice against the massacre at Casas Viejas, Sender was not in fact alone. Three days after the events, Eduardo de Guzmán and the Aragonese novelist travelled together to the Province of Cadiz (first by plane from Getafe to Seville, then by bus from Jerez to Medina Sidonia, finally by car to Casas Viejas) and, while Sender denounced what had happened in the pages of *La Libertad*, Guzmán did the same in those of *La Tierra*. As I wrote that chapter of this story, it had not seemed necessary to correct Dos Passos' imprecision, and the name of the journalist would not have figured in this book if Carlos García-Alix had not pointed out another of his works as the first of the clues that would lead me to Robles' murderer.

Guzmán, editor-in-chief of *La Tierra* until 1935 and director of the anarchist newspaper *Castilla Libre* between 1937 and 1939, reconstructed in *We, the Murderers* his terrible ordeal from when he was taken prisoner by Franco's troops at the beginning of April 1939 in Alicante until his death sentence was commuted in May 1941. The author does not hide the identities of some of the people with whom he was imprisoned (the poets Miguel Hernández and Pedro Luis de Gálvez, the playwright Joaquín Dicenta, for example), but the name and surname that Carlos had told me do not appear anywhere. Among the most chilling episodes of the book is the death of Felipe Sandoval, towards whom Guzmán did not feel very sympathetic: 'What little I knew of him before the war ended said nothing in his favour.' Felipe Sandoval, 'a cheap swindler, a common criminal' who had opportunistically embraced the workingclass struggle, underwent very tough interrogations by Franco's police in a Madrid prison. The other inmates, to keep him from talking, conspired to induce him to commit suicide. 'What do you hope to achieve, you swine, by betraying your comrades? What are you waiting for to die like a man? Throw yourself out the window,' they said to him every time he passed by. Finally they achieved their objective and, when he heard what had happened, Guzmán commented: 'No one is as bad as we suppose. In the end it turned out that even Sandoval had a conscience.'

But Sandoval had talked before throwing himself out the window, and his confession is preserved in the *Causa General*. This is an archive in which the authorities during the Franco regime gathered proof of what they called the 'red terror' to use as propaganda: it is therefore a source that must be treated with certain reservations. Carlos García-Alix, who had investigated Sandoval's story, got me a copy of that confession, from which one can establish the course of his life during the almost three years of war. When the military rebellion occurred, Sandoval was in Madrid's Model Prison serving a sentence for his participation in a bank robbery. Released after a few days, he was notorious for the pitiless way he ran some of Madrid's principal *chekas* (such as the ones in the Cine Europa and Bellas Artes, later called Fomento) and a 'special section' of the counterespionage services. His activities as a counter-espionage agent later took him to several other provinces, especially to Cuenca and to Valencia. In his confession regarding his time in Valencia, the surname I was looking for appears on two occasions. The first time it is mentioned as the 'appalling Apellániz, then factotum of the SIM in Valencia in spite of Sierra being the chief and Francés the general secretary.' The second time, after mentioning Sierra and Francés again, he alludes to the 'ogre' Apellániz, who, 'without officially holding either of the two designations, was the boss [of the SIM in Valencia].'

Sandoval's contact with Apellániz, however, would not have been very close, and his declarations merely attributed to him the unjustified detention of eighty men in a single operation, one of whom, a commander called Molina, 'they hanged in the cellar, and left his adjutant completely useless, and a third was taken to prison and they say he jumped from the top floor balcony.' Who was Apellániz? Who was Loreto Apellániz García, that appalling ogre whose atrocities could scandalize a man as calloused as Sandoval?

To find out we have to consult a book called *Blackmail of a People*, by Justo Martínez Amutio. Although born in La Rioja, in July 1936 Martínez Amutio was one of the principal leaders of the Socialist Federation of Valencia and, during the six-month presidency of Largo Caballero, he occupied the post of civil governor of Albacete, the main base of operations for the International Brigades. Loreto Apellániz was also from La Rioja and also lived in Valencia, but there any resemblance ends. Son of a protestant minister very well known in the Ebro valley for his kindness and honesty, Apellániz had arrived in Valencia during Primo de Rivera's dictatorship after passing the post office technical corps entrance exams with excellent results. At that time he was a member of the UGT Post Office Union and was a known Republican. Intelligent 'but with a strong character, haughty and impulsive,' his conversion to Communism happened before October 1934. His participation in the strikes of those days cost him two months in prison. It was through Apellániz that Martínez Amutio met Mikhail Koltsov, who had set up a company, with Comintern funds, to distribute Soviet films in France. Apellániz, who worked for the distribution agency, introduced them in 1935, and Martínez Amutio wrote of Koltsov that 'he seemed very kind and interested in Spanish things, especially everything to do with art and literature.' His activities during the war, though, led to a much less favourable opinion.

The three of them met again at the beginning of August 1936, when Apellániz called Martínez Amutio to tell him that Koltsov wanted to meet. *Pravda*'s special envoy was in Valencia on his way to Madrid, and the encounter, which took place in the Ateneo Mercantil, lasted barely an hour. By then, Apellániz, recently appointed police inspector, had already initiated a series of his 'innumerable outrages and cruelties.' Martínez Amutio says: 'From the first day, we knew he was receiving instructions from [NKVD bosses] "Pedro" and Orlov and that he acted with a certain autonomy from the Valencia Committee of the Communist Party [...], since they considered him well trained, as well as completely trustworthy.'

Apellániz's work was notable for its toughness, but also for not submitting to the control of Police Headquarters. This provoked more than a few confrontations with the Republican authorities. It seems that conflicts with the civil governor of Valencia, Ricardo Zabalza, were constant, and Martínez Amutio recalls a serious incident involving both of them. It happened at the end of 1936, when he received a visit in his office at the Civil Government in Albacete from Apellániz, accompanied by the counsellor of the Russian Embassy León Gaikis, the chief of the NKVD Erno Gerö (Pedro), and a Valencian Communist leader called Taléns. The NKVD had a plan at the time to create a police structure independent of the security forces and controlled by the Communists: the Offices of State Security, which would carry out investigations 'secretly and apart from all established norms.' The centre of the network was to be established in Valencia, extending from there to Albacete, Madrid, Ciudad Real, Jaén, Baeza and Cartagena; and Apellániz would run one of its sections. As soon as Gaikis had set out the plans, Martínez Amutio pointed at Apellániz and, alluding to some of his latest criminal incursions, warned him: 'Don't you go bursting into Casas Ibáñez again or any other village in this province or this military zone, and don't try to arrest or bother anyone without my knowledge and permission [...]. We're from the same village and we know each other well, you know I don't like jokes and much less the way you're behaving; so the best thing you can do is not cross the borderline from the province of Valencia to here.'

Martínez Amutio's words are important because they suggest that, in December 1936, the NKVD was acting in Valencia with absolute freedom, and he confirms this impression a little further on when he writes that, in spite of Largo Caballero's government's refusal to create the Offices of Security, 'a barrier for NKVD activity was established from the right bank of the Ebro on down.' In

Valencia, where Orlov's NKVD made themselves at home, Loreto Apellániz was the NKVD's man and Orlov's man, and this was at precisely the time when Robles Pazos was arrested and executed.

Of course, Apellániz's story doesn't end there. The Offices of State Security project did not go ahead but in its stead the SIM was eventually put in place. Apellániz, 'well trained by Orlov and Pedro,' joined the regional Valencia Headquarters, and his actions at the head of a SIM Special Brigade made him 'regrettably famous.' In August 1938, Martínez Amutio was no longer governor but was working for the Subsecretariat of Armaments, which ran factories in Linares. That was when the last of the personal confrontations occurred. Apellániz's brigade had just arrested a doctor employed in the Subsecretariat, as well as a technician and a specialist from one of the Valencia armaments factories, who were released after a long interrogation. As soon as the news reached Linares, Martínez Amutio travelled to Valencia, where he met with Apellániz and the regional head of the SIM (*comandante* Atilano Sierra, 'acting as decor') and demanded they prove the doctor's guilt and the reasons for the interrogation of the other two. Since they claimed the order had come from Headquarters in Barcelona, Martínez Amutio called the Commander in Chief of the SIM, who confirmed that 'it was up to those in Valencia.' In an increasingly tense atmosphere, Martínez Amutio managed to get the detained man handed over to him. Afterwards, with the support of the then Civil Governor of Valencia, Molina Conejero, he demanded Sierra's dismissal, which happened a few days later.

With a record of crimes like Apellániz's, his impunity could not last forever. At the end of that year, he made the mistake of arresting the socialist former mayor of Mérida, Andrés Nieto, who held the rank of colonel and commanded a division of *carabineros* on the Segorbe front. Apellániz was dismissed from his SIM post and a military judge issued an arrest warrant. He tried to dodge it by fleeing with the rest of the members of his Special Brigade to the nearby town of El Saler, where they barricaded themselves inside a previously requisitioned beachhouse with hand grenades, machine guns and mortars. The building was surrounded by assault guards. Apellániz only agreed to surrender to an authority who could guarantee that they wouldn't be killed. While they negotiated who that person might be, a company of *carabineros* appeared that had left Segorbe with the intention of freeing their colonel and teaching his captors a lesson. Seeing what was coming, the besieged hurried to surrender to the assault guards, who locked them up in the Monteolivete Military Prison (where Robles was probably held for a time).

The trial of Apellániz and his brigade lasted more than two months. Among the members who excelled at cruelty was a young university student whose father, detained for his supposed membership of the Falange, had recovered his freedom in exchange for denouncing possible fifth columnists. According to Martínez Amutio, this single denunciation had cost the lives of more than a hundred people, summarily executed by Apellániz's men, who 'beneath the veneer of defending the Republic committed countless crimes, pillaging and outrages.' The indictment only exempted two of the accused from capital punishment: the stenographers who recorded interrogations. The war ended, however, before the sentences were carried out. When Franco's troops entered Valencia, they were all found in prison and, according to Martínez Amutio, 'were the first to be executed by the *nacionales*.'

Another version, that of the Valencian scholar Francisco Agramunt, claims that the 'cruellest of the SIM ringleaders' was not arrested by the Republican military until Colonel Segismundo Casado's coup, in March 1939: then he was 'locked up in the Valencia Model Prison, whose warden, Tomás Ronda, refused to free him and handed him over to the *nacionales* in an attempt to be reconciled with them and obtain a pardon.' Nevertheless, the decision to keep him in prison while the authorities evacuated Valencia could have been taken by the socialist Wenceslao Carrillo, head of security in the Council formed by Casado. That's the way it is told in the chapter of Max Aub's novel *The Almond Grove* where he has Carrillo declaring his intention to liberate all the prisoners except for the few he describes as a 'handful of sons of bitches, murderers, blackmailers and traitors.' From an earlier reference we know he's talking about SIM men, and Aub mentions Loreto Apellániz explicitly and gives the aliases of another two, 'Pataqueta' and 'Esmolaor.' Someone replies that Franco's soldiers are going to shoot them, and Wenceslao Carrillo says: 'I'm sure they will, and first thing. Shame I couldn't do it myself [...]. One or two backstreet scoundrels fewer won't do the world any harm.'

Indeed, the new authorities promptly tried and executed Apellániz, who was shot by firing squad along with his associates on 3rd April 1939 at the Paterna firing range. The *Causa General* lists the identities of the stenographer or secretary who was spared capital punishment (just one), as well as the twenty people who were shot at the same time as Apellániz. Which of these identities corresponds to 'Pataqueta'? Which to 'Esmolaor'? I will not reproduce here the twenty names in case there is an innocent among them, but I will say there are several called Martínez, several called Pérez, a López and a Ramírez or two... None of these names reveal anything; nevertheless it is probable that behind one of them lies hidden the identity of the person who killed Robles. How many of those men were already under Apellániz's orders in February 1937? And which of those who were with him in February 1937 were involved in the murder of Robles?

The answers to these questions could hardly be found in the *Causa General*. The belated (and, as we shall see, irregular) official confirmation of the death of Robles – a Republican who was working for the legitimate government, after all – and the fact that his widow was not able to file a complaint regarding the case, are more than enough reasons to explain why Robles' name does not appear among the abundant documents deposited in the Valencia section of that archive. His name, in effect, does not figure in the list of persons 'who during the Red domination were violently killed or disappeared and believed tortured' nor in the list of 'torments, tortures [...] committed in this municipality during the Red domination.' His name does not figure in the lists of 'inmates of the Central San Miguel de los Reyes Prison' or that of 'inmates of the Celular Prison' or the

Model Prison, and this supports the hypothesis that Robles could initially have been held at the Monteolivete Military Prison, the only one of the other three jails in Valencia that fits Miggie's description (the two remaining ones were the Women's Prison and El Puig Monastery, located some fifteen kilometres outside the city).

What happened to Robles after his likely stay in Monteolivete? The *Causa General* does not contain conclusive information, but it does offer a few clues that encourage speculation. However, to follow these clues we first need to know how the NKVD functioned in Valencia. According to all the evidence (including his own declarations), the coordinator of the Soviet secret services in Spain was Alexander Orlov. Born in Belarus in 1895, his real name was Lev Feldbin, and among his principal contributions to Soviet espionage was that of having supervised the famous agents of the Cambridge ring: Kim Philby, Donald Maclean, Guy Burgess. Immediately beneath Orlov was a small group of NKVD officers whose trail is not always easy to follow. The most important of them was Leonid Eitingon, known in Spain as Kotov, who at that time was responsible for the preparation of guerrilla units; in July 1938 Eitingon would succeed Orlov in the Spanish NKVD leadership and two years later would arrange for Ramón Mercader to murder Trotsky. The first attack on Trotsky in Mexico (and a later attempt to murder Marshall Tito) had been organized by another of Orlov's subordinates in Spain, Yosif Romualdovich Grigulevich, a Lithuanian who spoke fluent Spanish because he had lived in Argentina and other Latin American countries. Apparently, Grigulevich's activities during the Civil War centred on the elimination of members of the POUM. As well as Eitingon and Grigulevich there was also a man called Vasily Afanasievich Belyaev, or at least that is what emerges from the testimony offered in *Men and Politics* by the American journalist Louis Fischer, who immediately identified Orlov and Belyaev as NKVD agents when Ambassador Rosenberg introduced them as Embassy secretaries. From Edward P. Gazur, an FBI agent who pieced Orlov's biography together in his book *Secret Assignment*, we know that Eitingon, Grigulevich and Belyaev were not the only collaborators close to Orlov. Two more names appear in this book: Lev Mironov, executed in the USSR when Orlov was still in Spain, and a certain Boris Berman, about whom I've found no other information.

Daniel Kowalsky, who devotes several pages of his book to the subject, claims the number of Soviet NKVD agents in Spain fluctuated between twenty and forty. On the other hand, according to the report by the head of the international section of the organization, by the beginning of May 1937 Orlov had two hundred qualified Spanish agents at his disposal. A substantial number of them operated in Valencia, and among Apellániz's deputies certain names stand out, such as *comandante* Justiniano García (who had commanded the Interior Minister's escort and in witness statements is often referred to as Justin), Commissioner Juan Cobo, who ran the Santa Úrsula *cheka*, and militia captain Alberto Vázquez, who was in charge of the Calle Baylía *cheka* along with two of his brothers.

We are obviously looking at a pyramid structure. At the highest point of the pyramid we find Orlov; somewhat lower down, Eitingon, Grigulevich, Belyaev and the other trusted Soviet agents; on a third level, Apellániz and his right-hand men; and at the base, finally, would be the rest of the Spanish agents, those shadowy collaborators who had to carry out the orders. The division of labour leads one to think that the decision to eliminate Robles was made personally by Orlov: dealing with someone who had been the interpreter for an advisor like Gorev, it would be unlikely for someone of a lesser rank to have made it. His Soviet collaborators would have been in charge of the interrogations, and Apellániz and his men of custody. Ultimately, once Orlov had made the decision, the Spanish agents would have put it into practice.

Let us now proceed to the clues offered by the *Causa General*. The previously mentioned account from an upstanding socialist like Martínez Amutio makes several of the testimonies contained in the *Causa* believable. Among them is that of a man called José María Melis Saera, who passed through two of the *chekas* where Apellániz operated (Baylía and the one in the former convent of Santa Úrsula) and who declared that 'Rossembuch, interpreter from the Hotel Victoria in Valencia, and the interpreter from the Hotel Imperio, Polit,' were also there.

The profession attributed to those two men immediately catches our attention: like Robles himself, they were interpreters. It should also be noted that the first of them worked in a hotel that has already appeared in these pages: the Victoria. It was outside the entrance to this hotel on the Calle de las Barcas where Dos Passos was collected to be taken to Madrid, and the novelist described it as a 'nest of newspaper correspondents, governmental agents, spies, munitions salesmen and mystery women.' That the Victoria was exactly as Dos Passos wrote is confirmed by Arthur Koestler in the second volume of his autobiography, *Invisible Writing*, where he speaks of a meeting he had with *Pravda*'s special correspondent, Mikhail Koltsov, shortly before leaving on an espionage mission. Ilya Ehrenburg, correspondent for *Izvestia*, also refers in the fourth volume of his memoirs to the Hotel Victoria, where he used to stay when he passed through Valencia. Ehrenburg says that the foreign journalists 'drank cocktails, played poker in the evening and complained of boredom' there and a little later adds succinctly: 'Sometimes a spy would be discovered in the Victoria.' Was Rossembuch that spy?

As we shall see, inconsistencies in spelling, especially in the transcription of foreign surnames, is common in the documents deposited in the *Causa General*, and in fact this Rossembuch would soon reappear as Juan Rosemboom Barkhausen, who was accused of espionage on 17th January 1937 and spent time in the Baylía, Santa Úrsula and Salmerón *chekas*. Félix Politi Caresi (that is, 'the interpreter from the Hotel Imperio, Polit'), also accused of espionage, was in these three *chekas*, and it is very probable that the case against him was prejudiced by the coincidence of his surname with that of another Politi who, according to a report cited by John Costello and Oleg Tsarev in their biography of Orlov, ran the Italian intelligence services in Valencia from 1930. The *Causa General* contains a reproduction of the entire text of Félix Politi's treatise, *The Dens of Stalinist Terror: the Santa Úrsula Cheka*, dated October 1937 but published a year later in Marseille by POUM Editions. From that text we know that prisoners at Santa Úrsula who were to be interrogated were called in between eleven and twelve at night, and that 'the interrogations generally took place in a place on Avenida Nicolás Salmerón.' Politi adds: 'accusations of espionage were never lacking, but were skilfully combined with thousands of ulterior questions. The espionage claims were generally so inappropriate they appeared ridiculous [...]. This part of the interrogation, inconsistent as well as crude, was later discussed in the cells of the former convent amidst jokes and the prisoners' sarcastic irony.'

The accusations against Rosemboom and Politi must have been lacking any basis, and after a few weeks they were freed. Robles did not have the same luck, and his final ordeal can be reconstructed by analogy with accounts the other two have left of their respective experiences. Which *chekas* did he pass through after leaving Monteolivete? It might have been Baylía and Santa Úrsula, but if that were the case it seems odd that neither Melis nor Rosemboom nor Politi should mention his name. Those were not, however, the only *chekas* Loreto Apellániz's men operated. There was also one in a house in Villa Rosa, one in Escuelas Pías and one on Calle Sorní, about which there are fewer testimonies in the *Causa General*. Which of them was Robles in? Whichever it was, the treatment he received wouldn't have been very different from that suffered by other detainees: long enclosures in a small cupboard, intimidating beatings, threats of being shot then and there.... With such routines they sought to weaken the prisoner's will and resistance: to prepare him, in short, for the nocturnal interrogation.

The interrogations took place in a *cheka* on Avenida Salmerón, and those in charge were almost always foreign specialists from the NKVD. Félix Politi claims the chief of those specialists was a Russian called Leo Lederbaum, who appears in other documents as Leverbau or simply as Leo. Juan Rosemboom, for his part, speaks of Peter Sonin and his wife, Berta, also mentioned in other testimonies, and says that 'the commissars and agents were Russians and Poles.' Among these was Scheier Hochem (who also appears as Jorge Shaya), a certain Muller, a woman called Nora, another they called José the Boxer.... These, of course, are assumed names, different from those the same agents had employed on previous missions, also different from those they would later adopt, and establishing their true identities is little short of impossible.

The only known name appears in the declaration given by a man called Jorge Pavloski Luboff, who was accused of espionage at the end of March 1937 and passed through the same *chekas* as Rosemboom and Politi. In his transcribed declaration he states that the boss of the *cheka* was 'a Polish Jew called Kinderman. Then he remembers a certain Belyaeff who was later also known as Weiss and then Blanc, a Russian individual of Jewish extraction sent by the Soviet government to organize the counterespionage services.' This Kinderman, who in other places appears as Shaja Kindemann, must be the Scheier Hochem mentioned by Politi. And Belyaeff has to be Belyaev, the supposed secretary of the Soviet Embassy mentioned by Louis Fischer.

Belyaev (which means white in Russian, as do his aliases in German and French) was active principally in Valencia, as is confirmed by the story Orlov himself told Edward Gazur many years later. That Belyaev was the highest ranking NKVD agent personally involved in the activities of the *cheka* is suggested by Jorge Pavloski's declaration. These two pieces of information could lead us to conclude that it was most probably Belyaev who took care of supervising the interrogations of José Robles in the Salmerón *cheka*. The interpreters of the Valencian hotels could have been a matter for Peter Sonin and the rest; but Gorev's former interpreter could only be handled by him, Vasily Afanasievich Belyaev, then thirty-three years old (and who would officially hold various diplomatic posts until his death, exactly twenty years later).

The murder of Robles could have been decided in a conversation between Belyaev and Orlov, such as the one they were having when Rosenberg introduced them to Louis Fischer. At least, that's how it could have been if Orlov had been in Valencia around the time that Robles was killed. But that was not the case. From Gazur's book we know that Orlov was involved in a car accident in the middle of January and fractured two vertebrae. On Sunday the 17th he was taken by ambulance to Paris and admitted to the Bergère Clinic, and was not discharged by the doctors there until the 21st of the following month, also a Sunday, when he was allowed to return to his home in Bétera. During that month, 'one of the most boring in his life,' he did not, however, stop working. The Soviet Embassy in Paris brought him daily communications from Moscow and Spain, and twice a day he dictated replies to his secretary. Furthermore, he remained in telephone contact with his collaborators in Valencia.

According to his own testimony, his usual interlocutors were Lev Mironov and Boris Berman. As I said earlier, I've found no information about the latter. However, we do know from Donald Rayfield's book *Stalin and his Hangmen* that Mironov was one of the then NKVD heads in the USSR, Nikolai Ivanovich Yezhov's 'staunchest henchmen.' Yezhov, in fact, sent him in April of that same year to Novosibirsk, one of the main cities of central Siberia, to pursue the peasants and Trotskyists exiled there (or, as Rayfield puts it, 'to arrest as many [kulaks and Trotskyists] as he could in the army garrisons and railway depots of the region'), and two months later, when Mironov was 'exhausted,' arrested and executed him. With such references, it's possible that, during Orlov's absence, Mironov took charge of the NKVD headquarters in Spain. Did he consult with Orlov by telephone about Robles? If not, a decision that in normal circumstances would have been referred to Orlov could have been made in Valencia, and Mironov would not have been oblivious.

However it may have happened, that decision was taken, and from that moment on the sequence of events becomes easier to imagine. One cold night in February 1937, Apellániz and his men received the order from their Soviet superiors and took Pepe Robles away. Where to? Undoubtedly, to one of the firing ranges the Soviets had on the outskirts of Valencia: the one at El Saler, or perhaps the one at Paterna (where Apellániz would be shot two years later). One of those must be the place where Robles lived his last minutes. Then someone fired a couple of shots, and between them they got rid of the corpse. Who might have discharged the actual bullets seems at this point a lesser enigma: perhaps Apellániz himself, perhaps one of the others....

My conversations with Carlos García-Alix offered a new hypothesis about the true reason for Robles' death, a reason in any case that Dos Passos could not have guessed. While he was in Madrid, Robles formed part of Vladimir Gorev's trusted personnel and, therefore, enjoyed the protection of the GRU officers. We know that, when the Republican government left the capital at the beginning of November 1936, Robles was one of many functionaries who followed it to Valencia. Alexander Orlov and his collaborators in the NKVD travelled to Valencia, and installed themselves in the Hotel Metropol. However, the main Soviet military commanders (Gorev among them) remained in Madrid to defend it from the siege of Franco's troops. By that time, a bitter confrontation between Soviet military intelligence and the secret services of that country was brewing, which declassified reports have finally brought to light but which nobody openly recognized then. On 7th November, anniversary of the Russian Revolution, Orlov and Gorev could still meet for lunch along with some others at the Hotel Palace

in Madrid, and from that meal a few photographs have survived in which Orlov and Gorev appear at the head of the table, one beside the other. But the hidden war between them (that is, between the NKVD and the GRU) would soon break out. The Russian military Commander in Chief, Yan Berzin, reproached the organizer of the NKVD saying his excessive interference would compromise Soviet authority and that he was treating Spain as if it were a colony of the USSR. Orlov, for his part, communicated to the Kremlin his unfavourable opinion of Berzin, who, he said, might be an expert in military intelligence but was not qualified to handle important matters of war.

By the time these reports were sent to Moscow, Pepe Robles must have already been dead. It seems reasonable to assume that at some point he would have perceived the tension between Berzin's men and Orlov's, but nothing leads us to suspect that he was aware of the risk he was running by distancing himself from the Soviet military and thereby losing their protection. Although there are no documented reprisals against other interpreters, could it be that Robles was a victim of the struggle between the NKVD and the GRU? In any case he would be an indirect victim. It is clear that Robles was not important enough to be Orlov's actual target. With his arrest, Orlov meant to attack Berzin and especially Gorev, whose prestige was only growing with the defence of Madrid: in fact, quite a few historians consider him to be the true saviour of the city.

By Stalinist logic, the move looked simple: by accusing Robles of treason, they were also accusing Gorev, or at least calling into question his judgement when it came to choosing his closest collaborators. The later careers of Berzin and Gorev confirm this supposition. Carlos García-Alix has followed both their trails, and the results are a couple of biographical sketches included in his book *Madrid-Moscow*. In May 1937, Vladimir Gorev was assigned to the northern front on a mission destined to fail. He arrived in Bilbao with his now constant companion, Emma Wolf, but the uncontainable advance of enemy forces then obliged him to retreat towards Asturias, where he would be rescued by a complicated aerial operation. A short time later he was seen in Valencia. At that time, however, he was already in disgrace, and soon, towards the end of 1937 or beginning of 1938, he was summoned to Moscow, awarded the order of Lenin and immediately shot on the orders of Stalin. His fate anticipated that of his then superior, Semyon Uritski, and replicated that of his predecessor, Yan Berzin, both forced to return to Moscow and shot.

The number of military officers who met the same fate points to a purge of the members of the GRU sent to Spain. The murder of Robles, in that case, would be just a prologue to that purge, and we may ask whether, once arrested, there could have been any way to prevent his death. Did what Robles knew about Soviet power at the heart of the government matter at all? Did the fact that he might have been indiscreet in some café matter at all? Evidence against Robles was not the issue, because Robles himself was the evidence: evidence against Gorev. In Orlov's strategy, imprisoning him in order to later release him would not have been of any use. What the NKVD sought was to cast doubt on Gorev by placing in his shadow the spectre of a traitor. Robles' liberation was ruled out because it would have constituted a confirmation of his loyalty to the Republic and, indirectly, of Gorev's authority. It is possible that his fate was sealed from the very moment he was arrested in Valencia, maybe even earlier. Robles was arrested to be executed and, perverse as it may seem, it was his execution that would become the principal proof of his treason. They did not shoot a traitor: they shot a man to make him into a traitor.

# 5

In their conversations, Joris Ivens had agreed with Dos Passos' proposal: to keep *The Spanish Earth* from being centred entirely on the spectacle of blood and ruins, they 'ought to find something being built for the future amid all the misery and the massacre.' The idea, according to Ivens' book *The Camera and I*, was to find a village that was 'extending the cultivation of fields as an immediate contribution to the defence of Madrid – people working together for the common good.' They found the village they were looking for in Fuentidueña de Tajo, some fifty kilometres from the capital. It was not 'a typically Spanish village' but offered two advantages: it was located along the Madrid-Valencia road and the inhabitants were constructing a network of canals to transform dry lands into vegetable plots.

Josephine Herbst visited Fuentidueña during the filming and witnessed these improvements: 'The seeds had already been planted, the little life-giving rivulets were watering onions, melons, and vegetables that some of the kids of the village had never so much as tasted.' We don't know whether Dos Passos was in Fuentidueña at the same time as Josie. What we do know from Ivens is that he was involved in the selection of the village and that he acted as

film
POPULAR
Argumento
ERNEST HEMINGWAY
Director
JORIS IVENS
Cameraman
JOHN FERNHOUT
tierra ESPAÑOLA
PEDRAZA
BLANCO
37
EL FILM DE LA LUCHA POR LA LIBERTAD

interpreter between the mayor and those responsible for the film. Ivens and Ferno stayed in a small room attached to the pharmacy, and the villagers told them that until recently they used to come to that place to pay money all through their lives: that was where the parish charged for baptisms, weddings and funerals.

Dos Passos writes about Fuentidueña in *Journeys Between Wars,* recording the fact that, since the local unions had collectivized the land (primarily vineyards) in July 1936, all the workers earned the same daily wage: five pesetas, plus a litre of wine and a certain amount of firewood. The mayor told him about other businesses that had been collectivized: the bakery, the lime kiln, the weaving of fibre baskets and harnesses. But they were proudest of the irrigation system they were establishing, and he showed Dos Passos the network of half-constructed canals. The writer took note of all this progress, but also that the division within the left had reached as far as Fuentidueña: the mayor himself, a UGT member, had told him maliciously that the members of the CNT local were 'small storekeepers and excommissionmerchants, and not working farmers at all,' and 'all wear swastikas under their shirts.' Even in the smallest, most isolated villages, could the anarchists not feel safe from slander?

He passed through Fuentidueña again after his hasty departure from Madrid, but probably didn't stop there on that occasion. Dos Passos already knew that part of the tragedy of the Civil War was the as yet invisible repression on the Republican side, and this was something that could not be reflected in a documentary, especially if the

Communists were in charge. His intention to collaborate on *The Spanish Earth* had weakened, although before leaving Spain he was still scouting possible locations in the Catalan town of Sant Pol. In fact, his name did not even appear in the film's credits, which attributed authorship of the commentary to Hemingway and the script to Ivens. The latter, in his autobiography, said only that 'Dos Passos had left us in Spain.'

The documentary was no longer one of his priorities, and Dos Passos was surely seeking to put some miles between himself and Hemingway. By 25th April he was already in Valencia. Ironically, that same day, the Madrid newspaper *Ahora* was extolling their friendship, dedicating a page and a half to them under the headline 'Two comrades from America. Hemingway and John Dos Passos.' Along with four

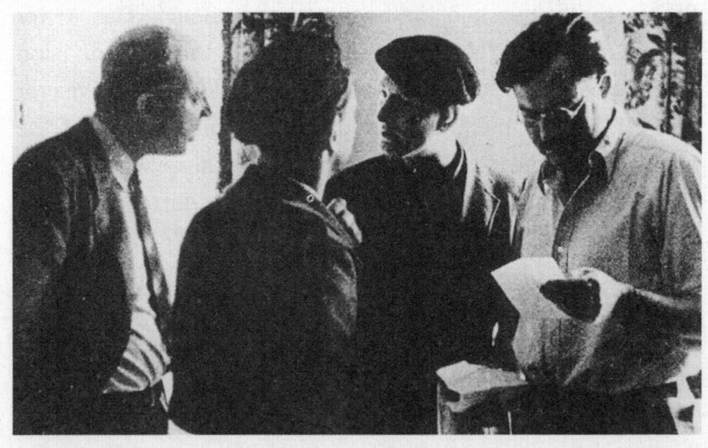

photographs (a front page one of Dos Passos and another of Hemingway, another of the latter with the journalist and finally one of the two novelists with Joris Ivens and Sidney

Franklin), the text was presented as an interview with both writers, but the only one who spoke was Hemingway, who referred to *The Spanish Earth* in the first person plural: 'We're thinking of taking it to Hollywood [...]. With the money we make from it we'll send ambulances and provisions for the combatants.' It seems certain that, by the time the interview took place, Dos Passos had already left for Valencia.

Dos carried on gathering information about the circumstances of Robles' death in the city, and very probably heard the same rumour Ayala alludes to when he says that 'in the end it became a well-known fact, but only by word of mouth, that the Russians had executed him right inside their Embassy.' Rumours, always rumours. When would he manage to find some concrete and reliable information about what had happened? As soon as the opportunity presented itself, he spoke to the American Ambassador, Claude Bowers, to arrange an interview with the Minister of Foreign Affairs, Julio Álvarez del Vayo. Although a socialist, he is considered by most historians to have been a 'concealed Communist,' and in one of his works he left a record of his annoyance at having to devote part of the cabinet meetings to arguing over death sentences. That same lack of sensitivity towards the life or death of a human being was undoubtedly what Dos Passos perceived in his second interview with Álvarez del Vayo, and what irritated him. Now Dos was sure he'd lied in their first encounter when he'd pleaded ignorance: the minister formed part of that shadowy conspiracy of silence and lies that had finally been revealed in Madrid.

If Dos Passos requested an audience with such a man, in spite of his reluctance, it was only for Márgara's sake, because he felt obliged to find out some concrete information about her husband's death. There was also the matter that Márgara had mentioned a few weeks earlier: the life insurance policy José Robles had in the United States, which could only be paid out to his widow when official confirmation of death was presented. As for the first, the minister was unable to offer any information. Dos Passos did not manage to find out the cause of his friend's death nor whether it had occurred in Valencia or in Madrid. As for the second, Álvarez del Vayo promised to make sure the Robles family received a death certificate. This promise was all the writer could offer Márgara when he went back to visit her in her shabby apartment on the outskirts of Valencia. By then, if we are to believe *Century's Ebb*, Márgara had also lost hope of ever seeing her husband alive again. Dos Passos hastened to leave Valencia for Barcelona, disheartened at not having been able to help her.

This is the moment when a character called Liston Oak appears in our story. By the end of April 1937, Oak had spent four months in Spain, three of them working in Valencia for the Foreign Press Office. We know from another of the Press Office employees, Kate Mangan, that he was a tall, middle-aged and distinguished-looking American, with glasses and long curly hair that stuck out from under a large beret. He was a chameleon, had been an actor and teacher and, though he insisted that he wanted to learn Spanish, he lacked a facility for languages. He suffered from insomnia, rheumatism and frequent headaches, spent long hours in bed and, like Rubio Hidalgo, preferred to work at night. Kate Mangan supposed he had come to Spain to forget his second failed marriage and, although his exact political orientation was not known in the Press Office, she thought he seemed to harbour some sort of sympathy towards the FAI and the POUM.

Liston Oak, as well as working in the Press Office, published articles about the war in the magazine *The Socialist Call.* He was in charge of accompanying (and perhaps controlling) Dos Passos on his trip from Valencia to Barcelona. Shortly after their arrival, Dos Passos and Oak visited the small coastal community of Sant Pol, where they were shown the fishing cooperative and a colony of refugee children. After a fine lunch of local broadbeans, fresh sardines and roast chicken with new potatoes and lettuce, they returned to Barcelona in the rain. A photo of Dos Passos and Oak was published in the newspaper *La Vanguardia* on 29th April. According to the brief explanatory text the American novelist, 'accompanied by the

journalist, Liston Oak,' had attended a screening of unedited material (undoubtedly, sequences for *The Spanish Earth*) the previous day along with the president of the

*Generalitat*, Lluís Companys. The *Generalitat*'s Department of Propaganda took advantage of Dos Passos' presence in Barcelona to arrange some press conferences for him. That Thursday he visited the offices of *Solidaridad Obrera*, which published an interview the following day, 30th April, in which Dos Passos reiterated his suspicions about socialism in the Soviet mould and his sympathies for the CNT: 'As an American, and one with libertarian ideas, I believe that the movement for individual liberty has great possibilities [in Spain]. The environment in which I live allows me to speak like this. A Russian *trust* might not be any less democratic than an American *trust*. We need to be inclined towards an industry that respects individual liberty and the rights of man. Real democracy in the United States resembles the anarchosyndicalist ideal in many cases.'

This was not his only statement to the Barcelona media. The historian of the POUM (then a young journalist) Víctor Alba records in his autobiographical book *Sisyphus and His Times* that he interviewed him in the Hotel Majestic. The interview took place on Wednesday 28th April, just before Dos Passos' encounter with Companys and, in fact, Víctor Alba, contributor to *La Batalla* and *Última Hora*, published not one interview with the American but two. In the official organ of the POUM he could slip in a declaration that would please POUMistas and anarchists more than Communists: 'There is no doubt that the revolution is helping to win the war.' On the other hand, in *Última Hora*, under the control of *Esquerra Republicana de Catalunya*, the only thing that attracts attention is the rather forced reference to the minister, Álvarez del Vayo, 'who has always given me all sorts of facilities. He is a man of great talent and culture, very well suited to his position.'

It is likely that Liston Oak was with Dos Passos when he was interviewed for the CNT paper and by the POUM journalist. It is certain that he was present when the writer met Andreu Nin in his office on the Ramblas, 'a large bare office furnished with odds and ends of old furniture.' Dos Passos took a seat 'in a mangy overstuffed armchair,' while the leader of the POUM spoke on the telephone sitting behind 'a big battered fakegothic desk out of somebody's library.' In another part of the room is 'a man who used to be editor of a radical publishing house in Madrid' and who can be none other than Juan Andrade, co-founder eight years before of Cenit and then a member of the Executive Committee of the POUM.

From this encounter came Dos Passos' portrait of Nin in *Journeys Between Wars*: 'wellbuilt and healthylooking; he had a ready childish laugh that showed a set of solid white teeth.' We also know from Dos Passos that he asked him about the Republican government's decision to take control of the police services. 'Take a car and drive through the suburbs of Barcelona, you'll see that all the villages are barricaded,' Nin told him, then laughed and added: 'But maybe you had better not...' Andrade interrupted to say: 'He'd be all right. They have great respect for foreign journalists.'

Dos Passos' text does not offer much more of the real content of the interview. For that we have to turn to the article Liston Oak would publish a short time later in *The New Statesman and Nation* under the headline 'Behind Barcelona Barricades.' The article centres on the division of the Republican forces in two large camps, and it should be noted that it was Oak who, after his three months' work in the Press Office, declared that the information about the confrontations between the anarchists and POUMistas on one side and Communists on the other 'was not often printed in the Spanish newspapers and it was, of course, censored in the despatches of foreign correspondents.' According to Oak, the anarchists believed there was 'a plot to eliminate them from the Spanish scene' and accused the Stalinists of having 'organised a GPU in Spain controlled from Moscow.' The article does not make it clear but, given the circumstances, it seems most likely that the activities of that Spanish subsidiary of the Soviet secret police were also discussed in the interview between Dos Passos and Nin. What Oak does say is that the Communist Party of Spain had become an instrument of Soviet foreign policy and that the USSR was seeking security, and willing to sacrifice the Spanish revolution, 'because Anglo-French imperialism demands it as the price of possible military aid to Russia against German-Italian-Japanese aggression.' In Nin's words, the only hope of saving the revolution lay 'in an acceptance by the Anarchists of a Bolshevik line of action.'

It should be pointed out that the article, published on 15th May – that is, just after the so-called May Days of Barcelona – contains Nin's opinions previous to that episode. The text reveals that the interview took place at the end of April and that Oak (and, as will soon be seen, also Dos Passos) left Barcelona on 2nd May, just one day before the disturbances began. One wonders what we would now know of the events of May if one of the greatest of British writers had not happened to witness them, and later, had not devoted the principal part of his best book to those events. Would they have met the same fate as those other confrontations, which did not appear in the newspapers, and were, 'of course,' censored out of the foreign correspondent's reports?

George Orwell's story is well known. When he arrived in Barcelona at the end of 1936, he was 'tall, very thin, horse-faced, out of condition.' (At least that's how the young Catalan journalist who accompanied him on his first walks around the city saw him. This was Víctor Alba, who would interview Dos Passos a few months later at the Hotel Majestic.) The photograph in which Orwell's head looms above the other POUM militiamen training in the Lenin Barracks dates from that time. Soon afterwards he was sent

to the Huesca front. His wife, Eileen, followed him to Spain a month later and worked in the Barcelona Office of the Independent Labour Party (ILP), which was affiliated with the POUM. After spending ten days in a hospital at the front, Orwell was granted leave in April to travel to

Barcelona and see Eileen. On 3rd May he was still in Barcelona, and he left a priceless testimony of what he saw and lived through on that day and the following days in *Homage to Catalonia*.

It was not surprising that shortly before then Orwell and Dos Passos would meet in person: after all, the office where Eileen worked was located in the same building on the Ramblas where Nin had his office. On the afternoon Dos Passos interviewed Nin he met Orwell twice. The first time, at POUM headquarters, they only shook hands; on the second occasion they had a chance to exchange a few words. This happened at the Hotel Continental, one of the places POUM men used to stay in Barcelona, and the hotel where Orwell's wife Eileen had reserved a room. In *The Theme Is Freedom* Dos Passos would recall seeing a face that looked sick and drawn and supposing 'that he was already suffering from the tuberculosis that later killed him.' They didn't speak for long, but Dos still remembered the 'sense of assuagement, of relief [he] felt at last to be talking to an honest man.' 'Orwell referred without over-emphasis to things we both knew to be true. He passed over them lightly.' In fact, he gave the impression of having understood the situation from all angles, and Dos Passos thought that 'perhaps he was still a little afraid of how much he knew.' In *Century's Ebb* he recreated the episode more elaborately, and in his fictionalized account we read that, until he met Orwell, 'he hadn't dared talk frankly to anyone. At first he was afraid of saying something that would endanger his chances of smuggling Ramón [Pepe Robles] out of the country and afterwards he was afraid some misinterpreted word of his might lessen Amparo's [Márgara's] chances of getting out with the children.'

It would have been in the Hotel Majestic where a crucial scene took place. There was a knock at the door of Dos Passos' room. It was Liston Oak, seeming nervous. Dos Passos let him talk. Oak wanted the novelist to help him get out of Spain. His sympathy for the anarchists and the POUM had made him suspect, and he even feared that Robles' fate might befall him: lately they'd been asking too many questions.

Stephen Koch has reconstructed this episode from Oak's testimony, exactly ten years later, before the Committee on Un-American Activities, and the essence of the story seems to ring true. According to this version, Oak met an individual called George Mink in Barcelona whom he knew from New York ('one of the leading NKVD thugs,' according to Koch's by now predictable characterization). This Mink, thinking Oak was reliable, invited him to have a drink and told him that, on 1st May, the Communist *apparat* was planning to provoke a rebellion by the anarchists and POUMistas, which they would exploit to justify the repression that would follow: 'Everything was ready. It couldn't fail.' This conversation took place just before the interview between Dos Passos and Nin, during which Oak could not help warning Nin of what, according to Mink, was being prepared. But Stalinist hostility was nothing new for the POUM leaders, and Nin, who would in fact be murdered by NKVD men two months later, paid little attention to his revelations.

In fact Liston Oak felt he was being watched and followed, and turned to Dos Passos to help him escape from

Spain. As Juan Andrade had said, foreign journalists were well respected and, in the company of someone with as much visibility and prestige as John Dos Passos, Oak felt his safety would be assured. The writer proposed that Oak should act as something like his private secretary and also agreed to bring along a volunteer from the Lincoln Brigade who had similarly appealed to him for protection. On 2nd May the three of them left Barcelona in a car the POUM had put at Dos' disposal, which neatly illustrates the transformation that had taken place within Dos Passos: having entered Republican Spain in a truck belonging to an organization linked to the Communists, he was now leaving it in a vehicle belonging to the party about to be exterminated by them. In *Century's Ebb* he recreates that trip from two points of view, that of Pignatelli-Dos Passos and that of the *brigadista*, who feared the moment they would arrive at the border because his passport had been retained when he joined the International Brigades, as had those of all his comrades. We may never know whether the novel's story of the Catalan fishermen helping the *brigadista* get into France was real or fictional. What we do know is that Dos Passos and his companions finally did arrive at Cerbère, and that only then could Liston Oak and the *brigadista* relax.

A few days later, on 15th May, Oak published his article in *The New Statesman and Nation*. Orwell didn't read it until, a short time later, he was admitted to the POUM militia hospital in Barcelona with a bullet wound. From the Sanatori Maurín he wrote a letter to the literary critic Cyril Connolly on 8th June in which he described the article as 'very good and very well balanced.' At the time Oak was contributing to various publications considered Trotskyist, from which an assertion of his ('the Stalinists in fact are today the foremost revisionists of Marx and Lenin') would be quoted by Trotsky himself in a text from 29th August.

Dos Passos, for his part, carried on to Antibes, where a few of the pieces from *Journeys Between Wars* were written. In the middle of May, he and Katy were in Paris. Dos Passos had not forgotten the Robles family. From his letters to Henry Carrington Lancaster we know that he wrote to Álvarez del Vayo from the French capital reminding him of his promise to provide a death certificate for Robles. The minister, however, did not reply and, in a letter to the then Trotskyist critic Dwight Macdonald, Dos Passos would express his disappointment: 'I rather underplayed the stupid way in which Del Vayo lied to me about the manner of Robles death. After all people act in big things the way they do in small; my talks with him about this business certainly didn't increase my confidence in that paladin of the workers of hand and brain.'

Dos Passos soon realized he would get nothing from Álvarez del Vayo, and one of his letters now in the collection of the Milton S. Eisenhower Library at Johns Hopkins University reveals that, to acquire the certificate, he would soon turn to other influential personalities: one of them was the US Ambassador in Spain, Claude Bowers; another, the Spanish Ambassador in the USSR, Marcelino Pascua, who, on a brief trip to Valencia, made time to visit Márgara to see how she was. Among these letters there is also one from Maurice Coindreau dated 28th May 1937 which verifies the American writer's scepticism about the minister's possible efforts: 'Dos Passos thinks he won't do anything.' A few lines earlier, Coindreau informs Lancaster, to whom he was writing, that 'in all these investigations Dos Passos had to be very careful. According to what he told me people don't dare to speak, watch every word they say. The Ministry of War where José Robles was working is entirely run by the Russians and it is most dangerous to work with them if you are not enlisted in the party.' And Coindreau cautiously asks Lancaster for the greatest discretion, considering that Dos Passos 'has many connections with the Communist Party and he might get in trouble if they knew that he has revealed what the Spanish government has done' to Robles.

I have quoted extensively from Coindreau's letter because it has a special relevance to the final episode of that ill-fated trip. Katy and Dos were preparing to leave Paris on their way to England when, on the station platform, they had an encounter, perhaps not entirely coincidental, with Hemingway. Frowning, he rushed up to Dos Passos and asked him what he had decided to do about *The Spanish Earth,* and most of all about the Robles case. Dos Passos, for whom, contrary to what Hemingway thought, this was not an isolated incident, answered that he would sort out his ideas and then tell the truth as he had seen it. They argued briefly about the misfortunes of war and the justification for war if citizens are deprived of their liberties. Then Hemingway, increasingly overwrought, wanted to know if Dos Passos was with the Republic or against it, and warned him: if Dos wrote about Spain as he now saw it, the New York reviewers would bury him. They would demolish him forever. 'I never heard anything so despicably opportunistic in my life!' Katy burst in, and she and her husband turned their backs on him and boarded their train. At that moment, Dos Passos' mind was made up: he would make his opinion on the war in Spain public no matter what the cost, even if he had to sacrifice his connections with the Communists, who had so much power in the American cultural media.

# 6

Although their attendance had initially been expected, neither Dos Passos nor Hemingway was among the sixty-six delegates who participated in the Writers' Congress in Defense of Culture, which opened in Valencia in July 1937. A month earlier a similar event had been held in New York, the Second American Writers' Congress, which Hemingway had attended but Dos Passos had not. In the inaugural session Joris Ivens presented two sequences from *The Spanish Earth*. When the showing finished, Hemingway took the floor to declare that cowardice, treachery and simple selfishness were worse than the war. Was he alluding to his old friend and the Robles case? Townsend Ludington believes that Hemingway was thinking of Dos Passos when he declared that, although searching for the truth could be dangerous, it was more useful than disputing learnedly on points of doctrine: 'And there will always be new schisms and new fallings off and marvelous exotic doctrines and romantic lost leaders, for those who do not want to work at what they profess to believe in, but only to discuss and maintain positions, skilfully chosen positions with no risk involved in holding them.'

The risk Dos Passos was willing to run was, in any case, quite different from the one Hemingway attributed to him.

Dos Passos was then writing 'Farewell to Europe!', which would be published in the July issue of *Common Sense*, and would register the ideological about-face that would bring him into conflict with the official left. All this, of course, stemmed from his experience in Spain, where a violent conflict 'between the Marxist concept of the totalitarian state, and the Anarchist concept of individual liberty' was going on behind the lines. Although Dos Passos still hoped for a Republican victory and recognized the organizational strengths of the Communists, he denounced them for having brought into Spain their 'secret Jesuitical methods, the Trotsky witch-hunt, and all the intricate and bloody machinery of Kremlin policy.' The unease provoked by what he'd seen in Spain was no less than that inspired by the attitudes of France and Great Britain and, just as he'd taken his leave of dehumanizing Western capitalism in 1919 with a reference to the high wall of the Pyrenees, in 1937 he took his leave of Europe celebrating the breadth of the Atlantic: 'a good wide ocean.' Dos Passos, who had sought refuge in Spain in his youth, now believed to have found it in his own country, which he felt had to be 'in a better position to work out the problem: individual liberty vs. bureaucratic industrial organization than any other part of the world.'

Attacked by Communist publications like *The New Masses*, which called him a 'tired radical,' his correspondence of that autumn reflects the intense debate unleashed by his article. To his old friend John Howard Lawson he confided that he thought the Communist Party was 'fundamentally opposed to our democracy' and that 'foreign liberals and radicals were very wrong not to protest against the Russian terror.' He must have had Lawson in mind when, in December of the same year, he published another piece in *Common Sense*. The title was 'The Communist Party and the War Spirit: A Letter to a Friend Who Is Probably a Party Member,' and in it he reiterated his accusations against the Communist Party, which in Spain had been determined to eliminate 'physically or otherwise all the men with possibilities of leadership who were not willing to put themselves under its orders.' Those who expected a retraction of his views were mistaken, and Dos Passos accepted the risk of being anathemized by the same people who for years had considered him one of their literary champions.

The novelist's position can be seen as characteristic of his personal consistency, but also as a challenge to all those who contributed to increasing the deception of which they themselves were the victims. Among them was Hemingway. Relations between the two of them were tenser than ever. In August Dos Passos was asked for his opinion about a fight Hemingway had with the writer Max Eastman in the editorial offices of Scribner, a fight that Hemingway himself had taken care to publicize. His reply was: 'Damn silly that fisticuffs for the press – in fact it makes you vomit.' When, in October, his literary agent suggested they might ask Hemingway for a phrase for the back cover of the reprint of *U.S.A.*, Dos Passos simply answered: 'Hemingway is out for various reasons.'

Dos Passos was not short of reasons for this reluctance. That summer, Arnold Gingrich, the editor of *Esquire*, had visited Hemingway in Key West to negotiate the publication of *To Have and Have Not*. The discussion was acrimonious because the book contained long passages that Gingrich considered libellous against three people, one of whom was Dos Passos. According to Gingrich, 'the parts that alluded to Dos Passos were harsh, and Hemingway admitted it.' In the end, Hemingway gave in to Gingrich's wishes, and made drastic cuts that included most of the incriminating episodes from the manuscript. This helps to explain the defects in the novel's construction.

A secondary character from the earlier draft of the book survives in the final version. This was Richard Gordon, who was 'writing a novel about a strike in a textile factory' and whose wife accused him of 'changing [his] politics to suit the fashion.' Although the allusions to Dos Passos didn't go much further than that, it's likely that the argument between Gingrich and Hemingway reached his ears. The confrontation between the two novelists about the Spanish Civil War was moving into their writings, and could be said to have remained there for the rest of their lives, even to survive them in their posthumous works. *A Moveable Feast*, published three years after Hemingway's suicide, included a savage depiction of Dos Passos. In *Century's Ebb*, which appeared five years after Dos' death, he recreated several episodes from the Spanish war in which Hemingway had figured as protagonist.

After Dos Passos' return from Spain, they only once had occasion to put forward their respective visions of the Civil War face to face. It happened at the beginning of the autumn of 1938, a few weeks before Hemingway's fourth and final trip to wartime Spain. It took place in the New York apartment of Sara and Gerald Murphy, who had been Dos

Passos' close friends since the beginning of the twenties and would continue to be until the end of their lives. That day Dos Passos and Hemingway went out onto the Murphys' balcony to talk and, after a while, Dos Passos came back in and commented to Gerald: 'You think for a long time you have a friend, and then you haven't.' Though there were no witnesses to the discussion, no one was in any doubt that the subject had been Spain. Did Hemingway again accuse Dos Passos of having a self-interested attitude with respect to the Civil War? According to him, Dos had travelled to Spain merely to sell articles to the media. That at least is what emerges from the letter Hemingway wrote to him from Paris on 26th March. In it he reproached him over and over again for feeling 'justified in attacking, for money, the people who are still fighting that war' and, rather crassly, took the opportunity to demand repayment of an earlier loan: 'If you ever make any money and want to pay me any on what you owe [...], why not send thirty dollars if you make three hundred or twenty or ten or any damn thing...'

It may be that Dos Passos had asked Hemingway to explain the attacks he'd been directing at him from the pages of *Ken*, a left-wing magazine recently founded by Arnold Gingrich. He had done so in June of 1938 in an article called 'Treachery in Aragon,' and again around the time of their encounter at the Murphys', 22nd September, in 'Fresh Air on an Inside Story.' In the second piece Hemingway mentioned an American correspondent, who had just arrived at the Hotel Florida from Valencia. From the first moment, the man had seemed convinced that Madrid was full of terror. Hemingway, holding back his urge to sock him, asked if he had seen any bodies or some other evidence of terror, and the other answered: 'I haven't had time to see it myself but I know it is there.' The confrontation took place in the room of an American woman journalist who was leaving the country in a few days, and the correspondent gave her a sealed envelope allegedly containing a carbon copy of a dispatch that had already been censored. Hemingway managed to warn the journalist of the risks that she would be exposing herself to at customs, and the disrepute that would befall the rest of the correspondents if the dispatch were published. That was how he convinced her to let him read the text, which, in effect, began by talking about the thousands of bodies found in the streets of terror-stricken Madrid... We cannot be sure, as Virginia Spencer Carr claims, that 'there was little doubt in the minds of most leftist readers that the balding journalist was a caricature of Dos Passos.' What we do know is that he would have taken it personally. It wasn't just that the description of the liar (tall, watery eyes, badly camouflaged baldness) fit, but the circumstances themselves evoked some of the tense encounters they'd had in April of the previous year in the presence of Josephine Herbst. Then too Hemingway had seen Dos Passos as a recent arrival who talked from outside sources, without direct knowledge of the situation. Then too his dissent had represented a serious disruption to Hemingway's circle (in that case, for *The Spanish Earth* production team) and to the Republic's image in the rest of the world.

As well as the agency dispatches, the script of *The Spanish Earth* and the novel *For Whom the Bell Tolls*, the Civil War inspired Hemingway to write a play and a number of short stories. The play, *The Fifth Column*, is set in the place where it was written, the Hotel Florida. Its protagonist is Philip Rawlings, a counterespionage agent who says he's tired and would 'like to never kill another son-of-a-bitch.' Of the five stories Hemingway published between November 1938 and October 1939 in *Esquire* and *Cosmopolitan*, perhaps the most accomplished is the first, 'The Denunciation.'

It is also the most interesting in terms of our story. The story is about a fascist, an old customer of Chicote's bar in Madrid, whom one of the waiters recognizes and, after much hesitation, denounces by telephone to the security forces. Perhaps this denunciation would not have come about if the narrator, a thinly disguised representation of the author, a friend of the fascist in the days before the war, had not given the telephone number to the waiter. The strange thing is that the ethical conflict moves away from a seemingly reasonable approach (do political differences justify the denunciation of a former friend?) to another, which is rather disconcerting (what to do to alleviate the remorse of the informer, who has done nothing but his duty?). Paradoxical as this might seem, the excellence of the story derives from its moral poverty. If the story seduces and disturbs the reader, it is because the reader is expecting the narrator to intercede to save his former friend's life. In the end, however, something very different happens. The narrator calls his contact in counterespionage and, after making sure the fascist has been arrested at Chicote's, says: 'Tell him I denounced him then, will you? Nothing about the waiter.' 'Why, when it will make no difference? He is a spy.

He will be shot,' the other answers, undoubtedly less tired of killing sons-of-bitches than Philip Rawlings. The surprise effect, rounding off an impeccable story, simply reflects the ideological oversimplification of its author, for whom the only good was what was good for the cause, and before that all other values, including friendship, were discounted. That contradiction would certainly not have escaped Dos Passos. Nor, of course, would he have failed to notice the detail that the person at the other end of the telephone, from the 'counterespionage bureau in Seguridad headquarters,' to whom the narrator refers the waiter, was called Pepe. One cannot help thinking that, while he was writing the story, Hemingway had in mind another Pepe, his friend Pepe Quintanilla, the senior counterespionage agent Dos Passos had appealed to when he was trying to find out Robles' whereabouts. In any case, the message Hemingway was sending Dos Passos via the short story was the same one as in April of the previous year: why worry so much about the death of an old friend who had been condemned as a spy?

When analyzing Hemingway's position on the Spanish war, however, one should not be too reductive. It is true that the writer, who lacked any solid political education, felt closer to the Communists than to the anarchists, whom he considered responsible for the military disorganization and quite a few excesses. But that rapport was determined by circumstances, and Hemingway, who gave priority to military efficiency during the war, would soon distance himself from the Communists once it was over. In October 1940 he published *For Whom the Bell Tolls*, whose protagonist, Robert Jordan, is modelled on Robert Merriman, chief of the General Staff of the Fifteenth Brigade and a former professor at the University of California, Berkeley, but also on Hemingway himself, who, through the mouth of the character, clearly expresses his idea that 'if we do not win this war there will be no revolution nor any Republic.' It was necessary, therefore, to accept Communist discipline, the only way to victory. But that was during the war; the postwar years would be something else.

*For Whom the Bell Tolls* is, as can be seen, a novel in code, and the real people the writer used as inspiration for some of the characters have been identified. We know from the husband of the interpreter Paulina Abramson (Jadzhi Mamsurov, a Soviet advisor Hemingway consulted in Valencia in March 1937) that the figures of the *guerrilleros* were based on the members of a detachment that operated in Extremadura: its ringleader, the indigenous Mexican Miguel Julio Justo, inspired the character of El Sordo, in the same way that the cook Shura, the mine expert Tsevtkov and the Andalusian miner Juan Molina Bautista inspired those of Pilar, Miguel and Anselmo respectively. The character of María, the female lead, came from a sweet nurse of the same name who had been raped by Franco's soldiers and whom Hemingway met in the spring of 1938 in a Barcelona hospital. Behind Golz hides General Walter, with whom the writer coincided on many occasions (among others, at the Fifteenth Brigade fiesta) and who'd been introduced to him by Mikhail Koltsov. The *Pravda* correspondent himself appears embodied in the cynical and intelligent Karkov, who, when Jordan asks him if many POUM men died in the Barcelona uprising, answers: 'Not so many as were shot afterwards or will be shot.' Another of the novel's episodes takes place in Gaylord's Hotel, where Karkov first bows to and shakes hands with his uniformed wife and shortly afterwards greets in the same way 'the well-constructed girl who was his mistress,' and then 'a man of middle height and a gray, heavy sagging face, puffed eye pouches and a pendulous under-lip called to him in a dyspeptic voice.' Hemingway does not mention the names of any of these three characters, representing Koltsov's real wife and lover (Lisa Ratmanova and María Osten respectively) and the *Izvestia* special envoy, Ilya Ehrenburg, who is mocked by the novelist for his naïve credulity.

Unlike his treatment of these characters, for some reason Hemingway preferred not to omit or camouflage the identity of the controller of the International Brigades, André Marty, who is shown to us as a bloodthirsty madman whose mania for shooting people is decried by even his closest subordinates: 'That old one kills more than the bubonic plague. But he doesn't kill fascists like we do. *Qué va*. Not in joke. *Mata bichos raros*. He kills rare things. Trotskyites. Divagationers. Any type of rare beasts.' Hemingway, who also recreated two cases of disciplinary cruelty in the Brigades in the story called 'Under the Ridge,' had witnessed the summary execution of two anarchist volunteers whose only crime had been to succumb to nervous exhaustion, and Marty's decision had disgusted him. By using his real name, perhaps the writer sought some sort of symbolic reparation for Marty's victims. His characterization of Marty provoked irate letters of protest from old brigaders like Alvah Bessie and Milton Wolff, who criticized him for having fictionalized Marty as a criminal, demonstrating that the writer's dualism admitted many nuances.

Dos Passos' reply to Hemingway's first attacks came in June 1939 with the publication of *Adventures of a Young Man*. The book opens with an invocation of the twentieth century, 'time of trials,' in which he denounces in an elegiac tone the decadence of the old values of liberalism 'for which we founded far from the world's thrones and principalities and powers an American republic.' Halfway through the novel, the author again takes the floor to condemn Soviet totalitarianism, which 'from the bloody cellars where they had killed the autocrat and the blotters of the secret police they salvaged the tools of absolute rule.' And in the final pages he directs his darts against the American Communist Party, which 'grew powerful and remarkably rich out of the ruin of freedom in Europe and the sacrifice of righteous men.'

His discourse had hardened since 'Farewell to Europe!', and it could be said that *Adventures of a Young Man* aspired only to illustrate his point of view with the adventures of its protagonist, Glenn Spotswood. He is a young idealist who, after contributing to the development of a revolutionary workers' movement in the convulsed United States of the twenties and thirties, ends up being expelled from the Party for putting his own feelings ahead of the needs of the Party. By then, according to Glenn, the organization's leadership had lost contact with the masses whose rights they claimed to defend and, faced with the belief that the ends justified the means, Dos Passos asserts 'that means are more important than the ends, because means mould institutions which frame ways of behaving, while ends are never in any man's lifetime attained.' *Adventures of a Young Man*, a coming-of-age novel, reflects the author's own political evolution, from the enthusiastic activism of his youth up to his later deception, and it is no coincidence that the final episodes take place against the backdrop of the Spanish Civil War, with Glenn having joined up to fight for the Republic.

Glenn's itinerary roughly follows the route Dos Passos had travelled in April 1937: train from Paris to a city in the south of France, car as far as the border, encounter with permissive gendarmes... Crossing the Pyrenees, it's not long before he runs into two old comrades from his organizing days. One of them is Frankie Pérez, who would be shot not long afterwards, accused of having put up armed resistance during the events of May in Barcelona. The other is Jed Farrington, now converted into a military authority, who refers to people like Frankie, saying: 'Our business is to win the war... They are interfering with our winning the war, see? My only hope is we won't be forced to clean 'em out before we win the war. We've cleaned out some of the worst of 'em already.' It is not difficult to recognize in the character of Jed, intoxicated by the great game of war, a likeness of Hemingway, and his argument with Glenn allows us to imagine what might have been said during the one between Hemingway and Dos Passos on the Murphys' balcony: 'You wouldn't try to make out these damn uncontrollables were martyrs of the workingclass?' asks Jed.

The shadow of the deaths of Pepe Robles and Andreu Nin

looms over the whole chapter, and soon Glenn himself is arrested by two members of the Special Brigade. After spending a couple of days in a cell, he is taken before a mock tribunal which accuses him of Trotskyism and of having participated in 'actively preparing the Barcelona uprising.' What is the accusation based upon? On Glenn's chance encounter with Frankie Pérez, by which he had established contact with 'this movement of counter-revolutionary wreckers and spies.' The similarities with the Robles case leap to mind: a tribunal on the fringes of legality, a trial without rights of any kind, a ridiculous accusation based only on the evidence of a casual and unimportant conversation. It does not seem far-fetched to suppose that, when Dos Passos wrote these pages, he was actually imagining the interrogations that had put his friend up against a wall in front of a firing squad. If Glenn doesn't meet the same fate, it is only because the advance of the enemy lines prevents it, and after a few days he is forced to accept a suicide mission. The novel concludes when he has already been hit by the first bullet: 'Must get out of this, he said to himself, and started to drag himself along the ground. Then suddenly something split and he went spinning into blackness. He was dead.'

In Paris, Hemingway had said to Dos Passos that the New York critics would destroy him if he made his view of the Spanish war known. That prophecy tinged with threat had begun to come true with his work of 1937 and 1938 (the two articles in *Common Sense*, the collection of writings on Spain entitled *Journeys Between Wars*, the publication in a single volume of the trilogy *U.S.A.*). Critics who had praised all three of the novels when they'd first appeared re-read them now in the light of the author's recent political declarations to conclude that where they had once seen sparks of 'proletarian hope,' now there was only '*merde*.' Dos Passos did indeed have good reason to fear the reception of *Adventures of a Young Man*, with which Hemingway's prediction would finally come true.

Samuel Sillen, critic for *The New Masses*, for example, thought the book was 'almost inconceivably rotten' and, due to its author being 'bitterly and stupidly' opposed to the Soviet Union, no more than 'a crude piece of Trotskyist agit-prop.' *Adventures of a Young Man* earned, in the words of Dos Passos himself, 'universal revulsion.' The novelist used this expression in a letter that summer to James T. Farrell, one of the few who praised the work. In his review for *The American Mercury* Farrell said the book's main theme was maintaining integrity in revolutionary politics. He thought the novel's negative reception was entirely due to political reasons, an opinion Dos Passos himself would have to share. In the same letter he expressed resentment towards the American literary establishment, which according to him was 'in a lousy mess.' 'The corruption of the Left seems to have infected everything,' Dos Passos added by way of explanation.

Of the critical reviews the book received, the one that seemed to hurt him most was the one, graphically titled 'Disillusionment,' by his old friend Malcolm Cowley in *The New Republic*. For Cowley, *Adventures of a Young Man* was the weakest novel Dos Passos had written since *One Man's Initiation*: lacking the technical innovations of the *U.S.A.* trilogy, his protagonist 'was simply not interesting or strong enough to carry the burden of the story.' His assertion that Dos Passos' trip to Spain during the war (and in particular the Robles case) had determined a point of no return in his career provoked the novelist to write a long reply. This letter to *The New Republic* is important because its recreation of the story of Robles' murder would become the basis for many later reconstructions. Edmund Wilson also answered Cowley in a private letter in January 1940. In it, after fondly recalling Robles, whom he had befriended in the summer of 1932 in Provincetown, Wilson questioned the editor of *The New Republic*: 'You promised further revelations [about Robles' supposed treason] when Dos wrote his letter to the *N.R.*, but they've never been forthcoming.' He finally accuses him: 'You write better than the people on the regular Stalinist press, but what you are writing is simply Stalinist character assassination of the most reckless and libellous sort.'

In his reply to 'Disillusionment,' Dos Passos did not attempt to argue with the objections expressed in the review. As he wrote in a letter around the same time, 'I don't think anything could be gained by arguing with Malcolm Cowley about my mental processes or what influenced them.' His literary prestige had begun an abrupt decline, and Dos Passos knew he was powerless to stop it.

It seems obvious that many of these negative reviews were intended as reprisals for his ideological transformation, and Wilson tried to console him by talking about the favourable reviews that had appeared in even-tempered Great Britain: 'Of course, the political issue has somewhat obscured [the book's virtues] for people over here. They don't have the Trotsky-Stalin controversies in the same acute way in England.' However, it may be argued that some of the objections the American critics raised were reasonable ones. Wilson himself, a man no one would suspect of sectarianism, thought the theme was good, 'but I don't think it's one of your best things artistically,' and partially agreed with Cowley in saying 'you haven't told them [the readers] enough about Glenn's soul (or whatever it is).' Arturo Barea's wife, Ilsa Kulcsar, who was a victim of Stalinist repression in Spain, showed little enthusiasm in the letter she wrote to Dos Passos on 15th July: 'I am afraid that the end [of the novel] is only too possible; but it is a pity that your young man could not have that great impression of a simple mass solidarity which I had in Madrid of the very first months – that experience which has helped me to resist the deep bitterness I felt, of course, when they began to hunt me down.' Read today, the view of the Civil War that *Adventures of a Young Man* offers does seem somewhat incomplete, and perhaps its greatest flaw is the explicitness of its message, that urgency to convince the reader of its truth and justice.

Dos Passos' literature would take more than two decades to recover the esteem of the American critical establishment. Eight years later, in a March 1947 letter to *The New York Times Book Review*, the novelist decided to make public his opinion of the critical establishment. According to him, in the New York press there was 'an invisible censorship of all books dealing frankly and seriously with Russian life and especially of books which do not fit into the pattern of thinking which our enthusiasts for the Kremlin regime have learned from the subtle and diligent propaganda fostered by the Communist Party in this country.'

He still held the same opinion in January 1953, when he prepared a declaration to defend his friend Horsley Gantt before the House Committee on Un-American Activities. Gantt, an eminent neurophysiologist and one of the people who introduced the theories of Pavlov to the West, was a professor at Johns Hopkins University. His friendship with Dos Passos had been the reason that Katy had gone to Baltimore in the spring of 1933 to have her tonsils out. This operation, we recall, was followed by an untimely bout of rheumatic fever for Dos, who would continue to return to Baltimore to be treated for his ailments and would, in fact, die in that city on 28th September 1970. During the witch-hunt unleashed by Senator Joseph McCarthy, Gantt's former links with scientists in the USSR had caused suspicion of Communist sympathies, something that Dos Passos considered absurd. In his declaration, the novelist recalled how his former interest in the Soviet experiment had led him to travel to that country in 1928, where he and Gantt met for the first time. Putting the case for his own later ideological about-face, he evoked the case of his friend Robles, although without mentioning him by name: 'My observations in Spain brought about my complete disillusionment with Communism and the Soviet Union. The Soviet Government operated in Spain a series of "extra legal tribunals", more accurately described as murder gangs, who put to death without mercy all whom they could reach and who stood in the way of Communists. Subsequently they smeared their victims' reputations.' His complaints about literary critics appeared a little further on: 'I have paid a certain penalty for my change in attitude because a leftist approach is rather predominant among leading book reviewers; the comment on my books tends to be distinctly less enthusiastic than in my earlier days, and characteristics formerly hailed as virtues have become faults.'

Dos Passos' anti-communism had been reinforced ten years earlier with another murder, that of Carlo Tresca, the Italian-American anarchist who in 1937 had warned him of the control the Communists would exert over *The Spanish Earth*. On 11th January 1943, Dos Passos and Tresca had lunch together in New York. After the meal, the anarchist and editor of the newspaper *Il Martello* went to his office on Fifth Avenue, and that same night, as he came out of the building, he was shot by an unknown gunman. Although the reasons for the crime were never completely clarified (the assassin may have been one of Mussolini's agents), Dos Passos always blamed 'the same gang that killed Trotsky in Mexico.' Six years earlier the murder of Pepe Robles had brought Dos Passos into confrontation with the official left; now the murder of Carlo Tresca tragically renewed that confrontation, and his increasingly fierce anti-communism soon took on a definitely conservative drift. Convinced that his country could be the victim of a Communist conspiracy, he at first supported, to Edmund Wilson's disgust, the objectives of Senator McCarthy and the House Committee on Un-American Activities, and only some time later came to disagree with its methods.

His conservatism was one of the reasons, if not the only one, that he became estranged from many of his old friends.

In his biography of Luis Quintanilla, the artist's son recalls that, when his father was in exile in the United States in the mid-1940s, the writer Elliot Paul avoided meeting Dos Passos. On one occasion, the author of *Manhattan Transfer* was in New York and telephoned Quintanilla's studio to announce a visit. Paul was at the studio, and told him: 'If Dos comes up I'm leaving.' Quintanilla chose to tell Dos Passos not to come that day, and their friendship too was thereby ruined. Some time later, when the painter was in Provincetown, he made no attempt to see his old friend; to find out how things were with him, he asked the owner of a bar Dos Passos frequented.

The novelist's growing isolation was greatly increased, in September 1947, by the pain caused by the death of his much-loved Katy in a car accident in which Dos Passos also lost the sight in one eye. The despondency that followed the fatal accident laid him low for a long time and, exactly one year later, he travelled to Havana in an attempt to escape his solitude and reclaim his friendship with Hemingway. After Katy's death, Hemingway had sent a telegram with condolences, which Dos had answered with an affectionate and sad letter. The encounter in Havana was the last for those old friends. From there Dos Passos sent Sara Murphy a local press cutting recounting the long and noisy farewell on board the *Jagiello* for the author of *To Have and Have Not*, who was leaving for Europe in the company of his fourth and final wife, Mary Welsh. In that letter he alludes affectionately to Hemingway as 'the good old monster.' In a letter to the novelist in June of the following year he calls him 'you old salamander.' It seems that some of the old complicity survived in their new relationship, but the correspondence between the two could not be described as abundant. In the letters collected by Townsend Ludington there are only two from Dos Passos to Hemingway, both noticeably brief: one is the already mentioned letter of June 1949, and the other, from October 1951, is a letter of condolence for the death of Hemingway's second wife, Pauline Pfeiffer, who had been a good friend to Dos and Katy.

In these years Dos Passos followed Hemingway's literary career from a distance, and his judgement on each new work was communicated punctually to Edmund Wilson. In July 1950 he wrote to comment on *Across the River and Into the Trees*, which he thought 'brought out the goosepimples.' He added: 'How can a man in his senses leave such bullshit on the page? Everybody – at least speaking for myself I know I do – writes acres of bullshit but people usually cross it out.' His opinion of *The Old Man and the Sea* was more favourable. He wrote to Wilson in September 1952 that, although it seemed to him 'a little too shrewdly calculated,' the more he thought about the novel the more he liked it. His comments coincide in general with the reception both books received: lukewarm in the case of the first, enthusiastic in that of the second; and most of all they show that his interest and admiration for the work of his old friend remained intact. There is no reference whatsoever in any of his letters to the Nobel Prize Hemingway was awarded in 1954, but we do know that in the previous year he had supported the granting of a gold medal to the author of *The Old Man and the Sea*: 'He is certainly the logical choice,' he wrote in a letter to Van Wyck Brooks.

By then, however, the last embers of their old friendship had finally been consumed. At the end of 1951, Dos Passos published the novel *Chosen Country*. One of its episodes featured a veiled portrait of Hemingway in a character called George Elbert Warner, who made propagandistic use of a scandal inspired by an event that had taken place in Key West in the summer of 1921, when a sister-in-law of Katy's had accidentally shot someone. The allusion infuriated Hemingway, and from that date until his suicide, in July 1961, there was no contact whatsoever between the two writers.

The news of the suicide reached Dos Passos when he was about to leave for Spain. That summer, as he walked the streets of Madrid that they had walked together so long ago, the memory of his old friend came back to him over and over again, and from Bailén he wrote a postcard to Sara Murphy: 'Until I read of his poor death I didn't realize how fond I'd been of the old Monster.' The wound that had opened in his heart in 1937 healed in the same country twenty-four years later.

The passion Dos Passos felt for Spain and all things Spanish had also been seriously damaged in 1937. The country that had seemed like the natural home of anarchism on his first visits had been living under a military dictatorship since the end of the war. Individual liberties, the defence of which was the core of the novelist's political creed, were systematically crushed by Franco's regime: the reality of Spain must have been painful for Dos Passos. His new relationship with the country had been limited to the occasional dealings with some exiles: with the Spanish refugees he helped in the early 1940s through the New World Resettlement Fund; with Julián Gorkin, for whose book he wrote a prologue; with Ramón J. Sender, whom he met again in New York and would visit at his home in California; with Luis Quintanilla, who in 1943 painted him disguised as a 'Sunday painter,' and from whom he would soon be estranged; with his old friend José Giner, who wrote to him regularly from his Paris exile; with Salvador de Madariaga, 'a gentleman whom I have much esteemed in many ways'; with Robles' widow and his two children, whom he saw on several occasions in the United States and

in Mexico... His refusal to return to the country he'd so often visited between 1916 and 1937 during the first two decades of the new regime seems illustrative of this estrangement.

He had been on Spanish soil in October 1941, but that fleeting visit was little more than a refuelling stop on a trip back to the United States. Only in the summer of 1960 did he decide to return to Spain for a few days. He did so again, this time for longer, the following summer, after Hemingway's death. Dos Passos travelled with his second wife, Elizabeth, whom he'd married in 1949, and their daughter, Lucy, who was then eleven years old. It was in any case a private trip. As opposed to the treatment of Hemingway, whose stays in Spain were conscientiously celebrated by the regime's media, Dos Passos' 1960s visits left little trace in the newspapers of the time: despite his anti-communism, Dos Passos would not have allowed his name to be used by Franco's regime for propaganda. Townsend Ludington has reconstructed his itinerary of those weeks during the summer of 1961 from interviews with Elizabeth Dos Passos: first from Madrid to Santander, later from Santander to Granada, skirting the Portuguese border, and finally from Granada to Lisbon, from where they flew back to the United States. Dos Passos had been in all those cities in his youth, and in all of them he'd been happy. One can surmise that the memory of his long-ago Spanish wanderings, revived by the recent news of Hemingway's suicide, might have spurred the conception of *The Best Times*, his book of memoirs, which he would publish in 1966.

The last time Dos Passos was in Spain, albeit briefly, was in November 1967. Taking advantage of a trip to Rome, where he would receive the Antonio Feltrinelli Prize, he stopped off in Lisbon and Madrid. When he died, three years later, the obituary in the newspaper *Arriba* recalled this final stay in Spain: 'Here he ate roast lamb and seemed still hale and hearty. But he was already forgotten to another new-born society.'

Dos Passos, in fact, had become a writer from the past. He recognized it himself in a way in his 1966 autobiography, when he realized that those had been his 'best times.' His political activism formed part of those times. As did Katy, and Spain. And Hemingway, of course, seen here in almost exclusively affectionate light even though not long before, in 1964, *A Moveable Feast* had been published, in which the old lionhunter took a cruel posthumous swipe at Dos Passos. The nostalgic though malicious tone of *A Moveable Feast*, in which Hemingway evokes some of the friendships of his youth in Europe (Gertrude Stein, F. Scott Fitzgerald, Ezra Pound...), abruptly snaps in the final pages, when the author, remembering a ski season in Austria, says: 'It was that year that the rich showed up.' Along with the rich, who are none other than Sara and Gerald Murphy, also comes Dos Passos, who visited Hemingway and his first wife, Hadley, in the Austrian town of Schruns in March 1926. But Dos Passos, unlike Fitzgerald and the rest, is not even mentioned by name. Represented as the 'pilot fish' who leads the rich

'sometimes a little deaf, sometimes a little blind but always smelling affable and hesitant ahead of them,' Hemingway's depiction of him is a striking example of perversity and rancour, not even omitting an unjust allusion to the murder of Pepe Robles: 'He enters and leaves politics or the theatre in the same way he enters and leaves countries and people's lives in his early days. He is never caught and he is not caught by the rich. Nothing ever catches him and it is only those who trust him who are caught and killed. He has [...] a latent and long denied love of money. He ends up rich himself, having moved one dollar's width to the right with every dollar that he made.'

It is not difficult to imagine the impact that reading those paragraphs must have had on Dos Passos. At that time he had already begun making notes for *The Best Times*, which, in spite of Hemingway's attacks, remains the story of a former camaraderie that Dos Passos always missed in old age. Their first encounter had been in Italy in 1918, when both were working as volunteer ambulance drivers in different sections of the Red Cross. Their friendship, however, was not really forged until they coincided in Paris five or six years later. From then on they shared endless experiences: the *sanfermines* in Pamplona, skiing in Schruns ('We were all brothers and sisters when we parted company'), the times spent relaxing in Key West, even a car accident that put Hemingway in hospital for several weeks... Only towards the end of the book, when the good times were about to end, did Dos Passos slip in a reproach to Hemingway's growing egomania, 'the famous author, the great sportsfisherman, the mighty African hunter.'

The penultimate paragraph devoted to Hemingway is steeped in nostalgia for the meals they shared in the summer of 1933 in the Casa Botín: 'These lunches were the last time Hem and I were able to talk about things Spanish without losing our tempers.' In the last paragraph, however, everything seems to have changed. He describes how, towards the end of 1934, he and Katy arrived in Key West and found a horrible bust of Hemingway standing in the front hall. Dos Passos began to make a habit of tossing his panama hat from the door and trying to land it on the bust every time he came in. One day, Hemingway caught him at it and removed the hat with an offended look. 'No one said anything but after that things were never quite so good,' writes Dos Passos. One might think the anonymous sculptor was in some way responsible for all that would come later.

# 7

But let's return to the Civil War. Back to 1937.

At the beginning of that year an Englishwoman in her early thirties named Kate Mangan arrived in Valencia. Unlike the majority of the young people then flocking to Republican Spain, Kate had not come to join the struggle against fascism. The reason for her trip was to rejoin her lover, Jan Kurzke, a German in the International Brigades who was recovering from injuries in La Pasionaria hospital, an old convent on the outskirts of Valencia. In June of the same year, Kate left the country with Jan so that he could complete his recovery in England. Later they decided to

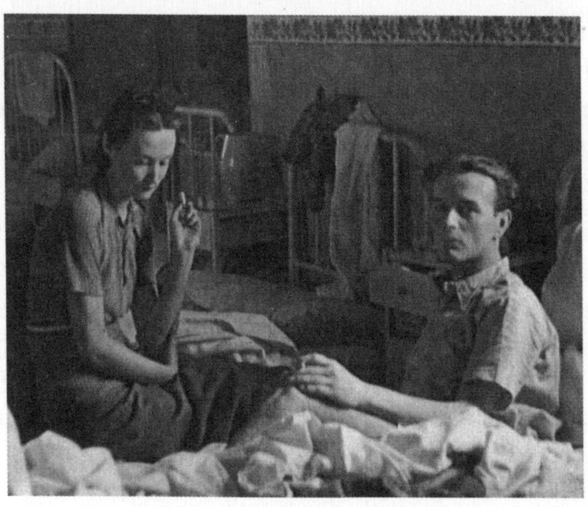

write together *The Good Comrade*, a book about their experiences in Spain. They would separate after the outbreak of the Second World War and Jan's internment in a concentration camp, but their daughter, Charlotte, has kept her mother's unpublished manuscript and managed to track down her father's.

Kate Mangan's testimony is particularly interesting because, during most of the time she spent in Valencia, she worked as a secretary in the Foreign Press Office. She had been given the job by Liston Oak, whom she had met through her friend and roommate at the Hotel Inglés, Louise Mallory. Her Spanish was far from fluent but, in spite of that, her superiors turned to her on several occasions to transcribe the speeches of the highest authorities of the Republic (Azaña among them) and to accompany and interpret for some of the correspondents who wanted to visit the Teruel or Madrid front or to observe the workings of the *Tribunales Populares*. But her usual work was carried out in the Press Office itself, and in her memoir she mentions some of its most frequent visitors: Ernest Hemingway, Ilya Ehrenburg, Egon Erwin Kisch. She met John Dos Passos only once. The encounter was not at the Press Office but on a nearby street corner, and it seems likely that Dos Passos (whom she oddly describes as 'yellow, small and bespectacled') had just received the news of the disappearance of his old friend Robles Pazos.

There were fifty-two people working at the Press Office by the middle of 1938, but at that time the number must have been considerably lower. The director was then Luis Rubio Hidalgo, who, according to his deputy Constancia de la

Mora, did not much enjoy attending to the foreign journalists who dropped into his department to request passes to the front, accommodation in the Republic's provisional capital, a place in some vehicle that could take them to Madrid or interviews with this or that member of the government. He owed his post to his friendship with Julio Álvarez del Vayo. The same thing, apparently, was true of Constancia. According to her own account, it was the minister's wife who, in January 1937, invited her to join the Foreign Press Bureau, although her official assignment, as her husband Ignacio Hidalgo de Cisneros recalls in his book *Change of Course*, came through the architect Manuel Sánchez Arcas, undersecretary to the Ministry of State.

Constancia de la Mora was called Connie because she had studied at Cambridge. Daughter of an aristocratic landowner and granddaughter on her mother's side of the conservative politician Antonio Maura, she met Hidalgo de Cisneros when she was twenty-five and her daughter from her first marriage was four. Her civil wedding to Hidalgo was one of the very first after the approval of the divorce law in 1932, and one of the witnesses to the ceremony was Juan Ramón Jiménez, whose wife, Zenobia Camprubí, was a good friend of Constancia's and owner of the handicrafts shop where she worked at the time. Elegant, multilingual and a fervent Communist, Constancia was ideally suited to run the Press Office (which she calls the Foreign Press Bureau in her memoir). Even Barea, who portrayed her scathingly ('the imperious bearing of a matriarch, a schoolgirl's simplicity of thought'), would recognize her organizational gifts. With the complicity of Valentín, her superior's assistant and confidant, Constancia gradually relieved Rubio of his responsibilities and took over increasingly large areas of power, until after a few months she assumed the directorship, while Rubio was sent to Paris to run *Agencia España* news services.

Among the office's personnel at the time, young foreign women predominated: there was Kate; there was someone called Gladys who caught Constancia's attention on her first day with her simple, fashionable clothes; there was a Mexican woman called Carmen who was not pleased at Kate's arrival; there was Poppy Smith, an American journalist who argued constantly with Carmen, who poked fun at her style of dressing.... But there were also a few men: among them, two Austrians called Selke and Winter (jokingly referred to as Rosencrantz and Guildenstern), Liston Oak himself, even the poet W.H. Auden, who, in spite of Oak's reluctance, collaborated briefly with the office and translated Azaña's aforementioned speech into English.

Also among these men was Coco Robles Villegas. Timid, lanky, with dark skin and very white teeth, grey eyes with long lashes and a lock of his black hair falling over his forehead, Coco had not yet turned seventeen the day Málaga was taken by Franco's troops. When the news of that event reached Valencia, Kate had gone out for a cup of tea at a nearby bar called the Wodka, on Calle de la Paz. When she returned she found Coco and Constancia de la Mora, alone in the office, both of them crying. 'Málaga?' she asked, and the boy, ashamed of his tears, nodded.

Coco's desolation was heartfelt. Like his father, he believed in the Republican cause. Also like his father, he had sacrificed the tranquil safety of life in the United States to devote himself to the defence of that cause. In fact, he could have returned to Johns Hopkins to begin studying for the Philosophy degree he had enrolled in, but he had chosen to stay in war-battered Spain.

His extraordinary facility with languages was undoubtedly the reason he was offered work in the Foreign Press Office: he spoke perfect French and English (his native Baltimore accent much appreciated by American visitors and colleagues), he could get by in Italian and Portuguese, and was studying Russian because he hoped to be sent to the Soviet Union with a diplomatic appointment. Such an aspiration was not far fetched. At that point, the Spanish Ambassador to Moscow (the first since the re-establishment of diplomatic relations) was the Socialist Marcelino Pascua, a good friend of the Robles family, since he had spent some time in Baltimore in the 1920s, furthering his studies in medicine at Johns Hopkins. It is safe to assume that on some occasion, as Coco told Kate, he might have suggested the possibility of assigning him to the Embassy staff.

Several people in the office were in charge of censoring the reports the foreign correspondents sent to their newspapers and wire services. Censoring meant making sure the messages stuck strictly to the facts and that these facts did not include any information that could be useful to the enemy. Once the censor had approved the text the request was put in for the long-distance phone call. There were only two telephones from which international calls could be made, and they were frequently engaged for official communications. When the journalist finally got into one of the cabins to dictate his article, the censor listened in from the telephone on his or her desk. The words were checked against a duplicate of the approved text and, if any modification was detected, there was a little key to pull down to cut off the communication.

But Coco's obligations at the Press Office did not include censorship. He was too young for this task, and in any case Luis Rubio and Constancia de la Mora preferred to entrust it to employees whose political affiliation left not the slightest hint of doubt: there is a very fine, sometimes sketchy line, after all, between censorship and propaganda. Coco's mission consisted, on the one hand, in serving as a guide for the correspondents who were arriving in Republican Spain and, on the other, in reviewing, along with Kate, all the newspapers and magazines, and selecting the articles that should be translated or summarized. He supported his mother and sister on his salary.

Márgara's consternation at events degenerated into a profound depression which, along with her weak state of health, kept her shut up at home for several months. Although later, in Barcelona, she too would work at the Press Office, Kate Mangan did not mention having seen her in Valencia. Someone she did remember seeing was little Margarita, Miggie. Tanned as a Hawaiian, with a bright smile, good skin and shoulder-length ringlets, Miggie would sometimes come to have lunch with her brother, and on some afternoons she would pick him up to go to the beach with a picnic of peanuts and apples. Circumstances had forced Coco to fill the void left by his father, and to develop a strong protective instinct. On one occasion he discovered that Miggie had gone to a bar called the Wodka with a friend, and forbade her to do so again. Another time they went to the cinema with an English *brigadista*, and Coco, to be on the safe side, insisted on sitting in between the soldier and Miggie. She was only thirteen but she looked a few years older, and everyone at the office was very proud of her, so clever and so grown-up. A fact that Kate does not mention in her memoir but that she must surely have known reinforces this impression: little Miggie, keen to contribute to the depleted household budget, had begun to work in the Ministry of Propaganda photo labs under the orders of Lladó, one of the photographers who produced images of the front and the bombings. Only Coco's concern for his sister's education could persuade her to leave the job and return to her studies at the school on Gran Vía Ramón y Cajal.

All through the spring, the department of Romance Languages at Johns Hopkins kept trying to find out what had happened to Robles. At the request of Henry Carrington Lancaster, a professor from the University of Wisconsin, Antonio G. Solalinde, wrote to the Minister of Communications, Bernardo Giner de los Ríos, who replied: 'The only thing sure is that there exists no record of him in the archives of the police, and they have not been able to find him in any place.' In a letter to Lancaster, Maurice Coindreau commented two weeks later that Giner had been deceived by the police. According to Coindreau, the Spanish government did not want 'any publicity and they would deceive *The Sun* newspaper the same way they deceived Giner de los Ríos.'

By that stage, however, Robles' death was no longer a secret, and Lancaster appointed the poet Pedro Salinas, who had gone to Baltimore to deliver a series of lectures entitled 'The Poet and Reality in Spanish Literature,' to cover his post. Salinas worked at Johns Hopkins over the following two academic terms. Lancaster's firm determination to keep Robles' position open for him is confirmed by a letter Salinas himself, anxious to secure a stable job in an American university, wrote to Germaine Cahen, Jorge Guillén's wife. In it, after referring quite inconsiderately to José Robles ('a fool who went to Spain, worked in the government on matters of propaganda and is now in jail because he's insolent and rakes the whole government over the coals') he complained of the failure of his intrigues to usurp his place: 'The head of the department has told me they are determined to wait for him.' In Salinas' defence it should be noted that the letter is dated 8th March, when the tragic outcome of Robles' story was not yet known in Baltimore.

How did Coco react to the death of his father? His pain and despondency were so intense that he refused to talk about the matter, and according to Kate, who felt enormously sorry for him, he sacrificed many of his plans and hopes: he gave up his dream of becoming a member of the diplomatic corps in Russia and, despite his sincere progressive convictions, resigned from the *Juventudes Socialistas Unificadas*. There are some doubts regarding this last point. According to statements that Coco himself would make in August of the following year to the judge presiding over his case in the military court, his affiliation with the *Juventudes Socialistas* dated from October 1937, eight months after the most probable date of his father's death. However, his sister Miggie, who did join the JSU, does not remember Coco being a member of any political group. The record of the extremely brief proceedings also states that, in July 1938, four months after turning eighteen, he joined the Communist Party, a fact that Miggie denies and which could simply be an embellishment by the officer who took Coco's declaration.

What seems beyond all doubt is his loyalty to the anti-fascist cause. This is illustrated by an episode recorded by Constancia de la Mora, who had assigned Coco to accompany the writer Elliot Paul to Madrid. Paul later called Constancia to tell her about a conversation he'd had with the boy, whose last name he hadn't known. Paul had commented: 'I don't know what has come over Dos Passos. I saw him in Paris and he won't even take an interest in Spain any more. He is full of some story about a friend of his being shot as a spy, some college professor from Johns Hopkins.' Coco had replied gravely: 'I hope that will not make Mr. Dos Passos lose his interest in the fight against fascism in Spain. The man he spoke of was my father.'

This must have been at the end of May or beginning of June. By then, there was no one at the Press Office who didn't know that José Robles Pazos had been murdered by agents of the Soviet secret police, that is, by foreign Communists who worked in close collaboration with the Communists of the Republican government and who, at least in theory, were under their authority. Kate Mangan says that the only member of the Press Office staff who dared to speak out was 'Poppy,' the American journalist, and revealingly she adds: 'It was obvious that our Spanish colleagues were miserable and quite helpless to do anything about it.'

Liston Oak's testimony qualifies this comment, however.

Oak claims that Coco's immediate superior, Luis Rubio Hidalgo, did openly defend José Robles' innocence, and that the Minister of State, Julio Álvarez del Vayo, also did so. Liston Oak's words do nothing more, however, than confirm Kate Mangan's observation about the impotence of her Spanish colleagues: they all knew Coco's father was innocent of the treason attributed to him, but not even the minister himself had been able to prevent his execution.

Coco's state of mind could not have been worse. The desolation provoked by his father's death combined with the grave dilemma resulting from the circumstances of that death. The Press Office was, in general, controlled by Communists obedient to the Kremlin's orders, beginning with Constancia de la Mora herself, who in spite of everything would not always be above suspicion herself. How could Coco continue within that atmosphere of rigidity and sectarianism, which justified persecution, while his own father had been its first victim? Undoubtedly there were moments when he considered the possibility of leaving the Press Office, getting out altogether, maybe going back to the United States with Márgara and Miggie. The temptation, however, clashed with actual circumstances as much as it did with his own wishes: with the gripping reality of a depressed mother and a young sister he had to take care of, and with his strong desire to contribute to the defence of the Republic. Leaving would have amounted to deserting, betraying his ideals, and what Coco wanted to do was to refute through his own conduct those who had accused his father of treason. If he kept working in the service of the Republic it was, ultimately, to rehabilitate his father's memory.

We know from Márgara's letters that she was certainly tempted by the possibility of getting out of Spain, and especially of sending Miggie to some safe place. Miggie's US nationality authorized her to leave the country at any time, and Maurice Coindreau as well as Esther Crooks, a professor at Goucher College in Baltimore, offered her a place to live. But Miggie was still a child, and Márgara was terrified by the thought of her daughter having to cross all of France alone in order to embark, also alone, on a transatlantic ship. As ever, there was also the problem of money. If the attempts to collect on Pepe's life insurance policy had been successful, it seems beyond doubt that mother and daughter would have left Spain. Possible destinations, as well as the United States, included Argentina, where one of Márgara's sisters was then living, and France, which was where Dos Passos had advised them to seek refuge.

The life insurance policy was worth almost five thousand dollars, but the Continental American Life Insurance Company insisted they were only prepared to pay if they were provided with a document certifying Robles' death, and that document did not exist, at least at that time. A similar situation affected the amount Robles was owed in royalties (around five hundred dollars) by the publisher of *Cartilla Español*. It was a vicious circle: Márgara could not leave Spain because she didn't have any money, and she didn't have any money because she lacked a certificate she could only get in Spain. In the case of the insurance policy there was also the detail that, to keep it active, someone had to pay the quarterly premiums. At first Johns Hopkins

University took care of this and later, in spite of financial troubles of his own at the time, John Dos Passos kept up the payments.

He and Lancaster continued to watch over the fate of the Robles family from the other side of the Atlantic. On 6th November, a collaborator of Lancaster's asked for help from the State Department, requesting that they demand a death certificate from the Spanish government. The reply came back from the State Department, speedily and unequivocal, very similar to the previous reply to a not dissimilar request: since Robles did not have US citizenship, there was nothing they could do. The money, therefore, would have to wait.

That same month, the Press Office moved to Barcelona and occupied rooms in the Ministry of State, into which the Subsecretariat of Propaganda had been incorporated since the disappearance, in the month of May, of the short-lived Ministry of Propaganda. The move coincided with Luis Rubio's replacement by Constancia de la Mora as director of the department. The Ministry of State had been installed on the Avenida Diagonal, then called Avenida del 14 de Abril. The Robles family lived nearby, in a flat near the Paseo de Gracia. In Barcelona, evacuees were usually assigned expropriated housing belonging to supporters of the rebellion. The Robles family shared a flat at 271 Calle Rosellón with Márgara's sister Concha and her daughter Paloma.

The first months in Barcelona were relatively tranquil. Miggie was studying at the *Instituto Ausiàs March* and taking an active part in the campaigns of the JSU: on two occasions, and at the request of the War Commission, she paid visits with other JSU girls to the soldiers of the Lincoln

Brigade, whose morale they tried to raise with talks, songs and dances. Coco, meanwhile, was still working at the Press Office, where Márgara was also now helping out, and both enjoyed Constancia de la Mora's affection and the protection of Álvarez del Vayo. The attention he now lavished on the Robles family seems somewhat suspicious, and can only be explained by a kind of remorse or feeling of guilt: his inability to save the life of the head of their family must still have weighed heavily on his conscience. But it is true that Coco, as he would later declare before a judge, was invited quite frequently for meals at his home and that Márgara would become close friends with Álvarez del Vayo's wife, Luisa, who was Swiss. In fact, Márgara, Luisa and the (Russian) wife of Juan Negrín, the president of the Council of Ministers, would get together every afternoon for tea at the Negríns' house in the distinguished La Bonanova neighbourhood, and Márgara undoubtedly took advantage of these encounters to bring up the subject of the death certificate. Her letters of the time return over and over again to the issue. The insurance company continued to refuse payment; their only concession had been to consider Robles as a missing person, in which case, 'if the insured has disappeared for a period of seven years, the beneficiary may take legal action to have the Court declare him legally dead.' Seven years: who knew where Márgara and her family would be in seven years' time? Lancaster and Dos Passos, exasperated, put the case in the hands of a lawyer, and meanwhile insisted to Márgara that she should put pressure on the influential people she knew. These, however, did not seem to be of much use to her: although Negrín as well as

Álvarez del Vayo promised on numerous occasions to issue the long-awaited certificate, in the end some legal problem always arose to prevent them from doing so.

By that time, Kate Mangan had returned to England. Constancia recalls in her memoirs that she had 'two large glass doors in her office and a large window.' When the sirens sounded they would move to the sofa. She was 'more afraid of flying glass than a bomb. The glass would blind you; after a bomb, there would be nothing at all to worry about.' The bombing raids over Barcelona by the Italian Aviation Legion, which had a base in the Balearic Islands, were then intense and continuous, employing a new technique of aerial terror: an uninterrupted sequence of attacks obliged the population to flee to the countryside or take refuge in the more than three thousand bomb shelters dug into the city's underground. The worst days were the 17th and 18th of March, during which the Italian airmen dropped forty-four tons of bombs and caused a thousand deaths. Meanwhile, the offensive by Franco's troops against Catalonia seemed unstoppable. On 8th April, while the Aragón front was collapsing, they managed to take Tremp in the province of Lerida, where Catalonia's largest electrical plant was located, and a good part of Barcelona was left without any power supply: the streets dark, the streetcars and electric trains rendered useless.

Coco Robles had now just turned eighteen and was about to be called up. On 20th April, two weeks before the call would come, he presented himself at the Francesc Macià Barracks and enlisted as a volunteer. According to his later declarations, he did so because he thought he might have some say in where he would be sent. Whether or not this presumed advantage had any effect, he was sent to the XIV Army Corps, which, according to the report by the Information Service of Franco's Military Police, 'consisted exclusively of guerrilla fighters.' Paulina Abramson mentions the XIV Corps in *Broken Mosaic* and recalls the names of some of the instructors, several of whom were Russians; but there was also a Pole, a Czech, a Montenegran, a Serb, a Bulgarian.... For a month and a half, Coco received instruction in the XIV Corps training school, situated in Valldoreix, on the outskirts of Barcelona, where specialists introduced him to topography and the handling of explosives. The school, according to Abramson, was well off the beaten track, and the soldiers knew the centre as 'the Red House.' That was where Miggie, in the company of some of her JSU friends, went to visit her brother shortly before 8th June when he joined the 26th Brigade of the 75th Division of the XIV Corps, which was quartered at Coll de Nargó, thirty kilometres south of Seo de Urgel, and operated in the Lérida Pyrenees.

The 75th Division comprised three brigades of a hundred and thirty men each. Their mission was to penetrate enemy lines by night and lay explosives (or, as they said, firecrackers) at strategic points. Shortly before taking part in one of his only two military actions Coco made clear in a letter to Esther Crooks how proud he felt to be able to take up arms to defend the Republic: 'I'm a soldier in the Spanish Republican Army fighting a foreign invader.'

The first action took place near Sort and ended in failure: they managed to set a charge but the explosion did not result in any serious damage. On the second mission things went considerably worse. Their orders were to recapture Tremp to re-establish the supply of electricity to Barcelona, and on the night of 28th July, after a march of more than fifty kilometres over mountain trails, the brigade tried to attack the detachment protecting the plant. Not only did they not manage to set a single charge, but the retreat was conducted in disorder and turned into a bona fide rout. The darkness of the night and roughness of the terrain undoubtedly contributed to the chaos, and among the various groups of soldiers that lost contact with the main body of the brigade was Coco's. With him were a twenty-six-year-old Andalusian soldier called Francisco García Durán, a twenty-eight-year-old from Aragón called Julio Lasierra Banzo, and two Catalans, Francisco Cerdá and Antonio Rigol, twenty and thirty-one years old respectively. After several hours of walking aimlessly they decided to stop to rest, and all of them fell asleep. And asleep they were found by a unit of Franco's army at seven in the morning on 29th July. When he was captured, Coco was carrying a Czech-made musket and four hand grenades.

Between 1936 and 1939, close to five hundred thousand prisoners were interned in more than one hundred concentration camps. Franco's general staff intended to create a fixed network of camps, in which to lock up 'enemies of Spain' and submit them to ideological, moral and religious re-education programmes. However, the growing influx of prisoners and the dynamic of the war itself pushed the system to the brink of collapse and led to the triumph of improvisation. This meant that the rights guaranteed in the Geneva Conventions of 1929, which in theory should have applied, were very seldom respected. In many of those camps the number of inmates was three times the maximum capacity, and there were many instances when the Inspectors of Prisoner Concentration Camps recommended the closure of some of them due to lack of water and latrines. Bedbugs and fleas infested the barracks in which the prisoners were crowded together, and they had to disinfect their clothing by washing it in boiling water. The insanitary conditions were made worse by bad food, the direct cause of death for a large number of prisoners. The daily diet usually consisted of broth made of potato peelings, along with a tiny piece of bread, or a couple of tins of sardines. Only those who received food from their families escaped malnutrition, and transfer to a camp far from one's own province was in many cases a death sentence. Those who survived the hunger (and typhus, which ravaged the prison population) waited to be sent to jail, military service, forced labour or in front of the firing squad.

Near the city of Zaragoza, owing to its proximity to some of the most active and long-lasting fronts of the conflict, there were two large concentration camps almost side by side: one in San Juan de Mozarrifar and the other in the grounds of the General Military Academy in San Gregorio. The San Gregorio camp existed from the beginning of the war; the one in San Juan, through which more than eighty thousand prisoners passed, came into being in February 1938 due to the overpopulation of the first. Both of them were in zones of sparse vegetation, with no shade to alleviate the asphyxiating heat of the Aragón summer. Coco was sent to the San Gregorio camp the day he was captured and, very shortly afterwards, faced a summary military tribunal.

With the customary rhetoric of Franco's military prosecutors, who considered those who defended the legally established Republican regime to be rebels, he was accused of adherence to the rebellion. His statement was taken on 13th August. Coco, true to his principles, declared that he had never had any intention to go over to the *nacionales* and that he firmly believed in the final victory of the Republican side. Later he asked that his good friend Julio Álvarez del Vayo be informed of his detention, hoping he would begin negotiations for a possible prisoner exchange. This can only be seen as a sign of naivety: first, because prisoner swaps were very rare (Franco, in fact, always stated his total opposition to any projected exchange except in the case of Germans and Italians, no doubt due to the demands of his allies); and secondly, because Álvarez del Vayo, who had been unable to prevent the murder of Coco's father by persons supposedly under the authority of his government, could hardly be expected to influence the rival government to ensure a better fate for the son.

The death of Robles Pazos, furthermore, not only would not aid his son's defence but threatened to turn into a serious aggravating factor: in the 19th August minutes of the Classification Commission of Prisoners and Presentados, written in crude barracks prose, Coco was considered 'a powerful auxiliary of the Rebellion, being *paradógica* (paradocksical) [sic] this collaboration after the murder of his father, which shows him as having degraded morals.' Given Coco's slight political importance, this must have been one of the determining factors in the Commission's unanimous decision to include him in section C, which meant 'hostile to the Regime' and which was used to classify politicians, commanding officers of the Republican Army or the Popular Front and labour leaders.

The steadfast Republican convictions José Robles had held and which Coco now demonstrated were likewise shared by the youngest member of the family. In the middle of August 1938, Miggie travelled by way of Paris and Le Havre to the United States in order to participate in the Second World Youth Congress, celebrated at Vassar College, in Poughkeepsie, New York. She was the youngest member of

the delegation, which also included Teresa Pàmies, who in time would become a prominent Catalan writer. Four young men travelled with the two girls, including Ricardo Muñoz Suay, later a prestigious screenwriter, and Manuel Azcárate, member of an illustrious family of Republican politicians linked to the *Institución Libre de Enseñanza*.

A friend in England, who was aware of my investigations, told me about a Channel 4 television programme on the Spanish Civil War in which Miggie Robles' involvement in this event was mentioned. The participant who spoke of Miggie was Teresa Pàmies, who remembered the day they were visited by the honorary president of the Congress, Eleanor Roosevelt. She showed genuine concern over the bombardment of defenceless cities and over the terrible situation of the children, and out of all the young delegates seated around the First Lady, it was little Miggie who decided to speak up and ask why her government did not lift the blockade against the Spanish Republic. 'There was a long silence. Later, Mrs Roosevelt, smiling as if she expected a round of applause, said that she was not a member of the government. No one applauded.'

The Congress took place during the second half of August. Along with the delegations from other countries, the Spanish, which excluded the youth section of the POUM but did include anarchists, arrived by ship at the river port of Poughkeepsie. A band was waiting there to welcome them by playing their respective national anthems. However, the musicians had out-of-date sheet music and started playing the first chords of *The Royal March*: the indignation of the young Spaniards was so great that, as Manuel Azcárate recalls in his memoirs, 'the musicians were in danger of being dunked in the Hudson.' Azcárate was there as a representative of the JSU, and his instructions were to 'speak only of peace and the struggle against Franco.' The objective was to create a broad front for peace against fascism, and for that reason it would not do to frighten a public as anti-Communist as that of the United States. That is why the young Communists did not object to the participation in the Congress of some conservative organizations, like the Young Men's Christian Association.

Ricardo Muñoz Suay and Miggie Robles represented the University Students Federation, and Teresa Pàmies the Unified Socialist Youth of Catalonia. The delegates stayed in the university residences and, as well as participating in the various colloquial discussions and granting interviews to journalists, they met committees and associations in solidarity with the Republic. At one of those events they attended a showing of *The Spanish Earth*, the film that, a year and a half earlier, had been the reason for Dos Passos' last trip to Spain. Another of their missions, of course, was to try to raise funds for the cause. One of the initiatives consisted in selling albums to support Spanish children. These booklets were to be filled in by the buyer with little stamps with the image of a child, one for each week and, to judge by the date of the last square, the resistance of the troops loyal to the Republic was to extend at least until the middle of September, revealing an optimism that reality would soon refute. The photograph that illustrated the album showed two smiling girls on the deck of a ship holding a Republican flag. Those two girls were Miggie Robles and Teresa Pàmies.

Pàmies would also evoke this episode in an autobiographical book, *Quan érem capitans*. The hopes the Republican leaders had invested in the possible repercussions of the propaganda were expressed by José Giral, then minister without portfolio, who declared to the press that

the Spanish youth should take to America 'the energetic and aching voice of our tragedy, the manly shout of our enthusiasm.' Shortly before their departure, President Azaña received the delegation in his office in Pedralbes and, on their way through Paris, Marcelino Pascua would do the same at the Spanish Embassy. In *When We Were Captains* Teresa Pàmies also relates how, at the border crossing of Puigcerdà, some anarchist women customs officials submitted Miggie and her to an extremely thorough search and that, when they were at Vassar College, there was a bit of a stir when 'a southern journalist' discovered that the father of her companion had 'disappeared' in Republican Spain. 'Poor Miggie,' adds the Catalan writer, 'was besieged by journalists asking questions she could not answer.'

The discovery of these accounts was providential for my investigation. Thanks to Teresa Pàmies and her son, the writer Sergi Pàmies, I got the telephone number of the family of Manuel Azcárate, who had recently died. When I called, his daughter Carmen told me about one of her uncles, Luis Azcárate, who had been living for the last twenty years with a cultured and charming woman originally from Baltimore. This turned out to be Margarita Robles Villegas, Miggie, for whom I had searched painstakingly and fruitlessly through the groups of Republican exiles in Mexico, and who had been living for some time in Seville. Miggie and Luis had fallen in love in Paris in 1939. Although they saw each other again a short while later in Mexico, fate took them in different directions, and they did not meet again until 1983. By then Miggie had been widowed for two years. While she had four children, he had three. Miggie and Luis immediately resumed a love story that had been postponed forty-four years earlier. They lived together

in Mexico City, in Seville, in a tiny village in Provence, in Casablanca, until in 1995 they returned to Seville to settle down for good. I visited them for the first time at the beginning of March 2003, and it goes without saying that much of the information contained in this book comes directly from Miggie's exceptional memory.

Let us return once again to 1938 and to the proceedings against Coco Robles. By then, the San Gregorio camp was no longer used for internment but as a classification centre: there, according to the historian Javier Rodrigo in *The Concentration Camps of Franco's Spain*, 'the first interrogations were carried out, the first requests for references, the first tortures, the first mistreatments.' In the middle of September, once classified as hostile to the regime, Coco was transferred to San Juan de Mozarrifar. The central building of this camp was an old paper factory and, at least for a time, was without sanitation or plumbing. The villagers remember seeing the prisoners marched down in formation to wash in the River Gállego. On the way back, they had to carry rocks from the river bed that would later be used to construct the camp. The prisoners' work consisted, therefore, in building their own jail: they positioned windows, installed electrical wiring, laid out barbed wire around the perimeter of the camp. The obligation to form up was imposed not only when they went to bathe: they also had to fall in every morning to raise the flag and at dusk to lower it, and twice more for the dishing out of food and the headcount. On Sundays, they had to line up to go to mass, and on other days, in the rare moments they weren't working, they had to attend 'patriotic lectures' intended to avert the risk of 'injurious idleness,' lectures that dealt with subjects such as the errors of the class struggle, the prevailing criminality before 18th July or the objectives of Judaism, Freemasonry and Marxism. These were not the only duties imposed by the process of re-education: the prisoners also had to give straight-arm salutes, sing fascist anthems and shout fascist slogans. One statement reproduced by Javier Rodrigo indicates that in the San Juan de Mozarrifar camp the instruction was that 'in nationalist Spain prisoners saluted with arms outstretched hailing Franco and bareheaded.' Those who disobeyed were exposed to greater cruelties and humiliations. Another witness describes the 'punishments not sanctioned by the Military Code of Justice,' such as tying prisoners by their feet and hands to a tree or an electricity pylon, or suspending them from the roof by a rope for two hours.

On 29th September 1938, Coco Robles reaffirmed his statements and insisted that negotiations be opened to arrange his exchange. On 4th October he had a medical examination by the camp's medic, who certified that he was not suffering from 'any illness or physical defect.' On 16th November he was notified that the death penalty was being sought in his case. Coco, seemingly resigned to a fate shared with many of his comrades in adversity, declined to make any declarations, and on 10th December the military tribunal condemned him to death, 'with corresponding prison sentence in case of reprieve and payment of civil responsibility to be set at an unspecified amount.'

It must have been around this date that he was transferred out of the concentration camp, where the risk of escape was high, to a more secure prison. Without notice, he was tied to a line of prisoners and driven to the Provincial Prison of Zaragoza, in the neighbourhood of Torrero. The hygienic and sanitary conditions were no better in the prisons than in the concentration camps. From *In the Prisons of Spain* by the Aragonese anarchist Ramón Rufat, who spent two and a half years with Coco in Torrero, we know that most of the prisoners had scabies, and the most seriously ill were confined in a disgusting corridor, 'with a terrible smell all day of a sulphur mixture they called sulfureti, which they smeared over the whole body.' In any case, scabies was not the worst of their problems. During the final year of the war and the first of the postwar period, the overcrowding in the Zaragoza jail reached unimaginable extremes. Though designed to house two hundred and fifty inmates, at one point the population reached more than six thousand, and Rufat recalls that, inside the prison, 'the notion of space did not exist: no one could move without having to step on and push a dozen others.' On every square metre of the floor no fewer than five men slept, and 'some beds had been made right on top of the toilets, with doors ripped from the walls laid on top of them.' Not even when they were taken out to the patio did the situation improve: there too there was still 'not enough room for a pin,' and it didn't matter if they were ordered to fall out: there wasn't enough room to walk or even stretch one's legs.

It might be thought that Rufat's testimony was an exaggeration if it were not confirmed by that of the Capuchin priest Gumersindo de Estella. He was chaplain of the Zaragoza prison from June 1937 to March 1942, and his main task was to minister to the accused before they were shot against the walls of the nearby Torrero cemetery. At that time, Father Gumersindo de Estella, whose real name was Martín Zubeldía Inda, kept a secret diary where he wrote that 'in many individual cells there were eighteen prisoners locked up.' Both the anarchist and the priest pointed out the extremely inhuman treatment the guards meted out to the inmates. Rufat says that Zaragoza had 'the worst prison by reputation and in fact.' What seems most striking is that the abuse was inflicted not by the few members of staff (only eleven for the whole prison) but by 'the prisoners themselves who established themselves as petty bosses and their many assistants.' Gumersindo de Estella regretted that the beatings 'were frequent every day, cruelly dealt by these gang leaders, who tended to be inmates condemned to many years of prison for common crimes.' One of his commentaries on the comportment of these individuals is revealing of the atmosphere that prevailed in the prison: 'the less sensitive and crueller one showed oneself to be, the more one was considered a supporter of Franco.'

By the time Coco was sent to the Torrero jail, his confidence in military victory must have begun to flag. The end of November saw the collapse of the Ebro campaign, in which the Republican forces had invested their last hopes, and Franco's troops prepared to embark on one last offensive before the one they designated the 'Victory' campaign. Coco's mother and sister were still in Barcelona waiting for news, and the news they received could not have been more demoralizing. The people of Barcelona, many of them refugees who had grown accustomed to fleeing, saw the

Republican troops pass through in retreat, and widespread panic made calls for resistance futile. Franco's scouting parties entered the city on the morning of 26th January 1939. On the following day General Yagüe presided over a huge open-air mass in the Plaza de Cataluña. At that moment, Márgara Villegas and her daughter had just left Barcelona in haste, along with several thousand other people, and were walking the hundred and thirty kilometres to Figueras, the short-lived Republican capital.

It took them four days to get there. In Barcelona, before they left, they went to the offices of the JSU, in the Hotel Colón on the Plaza de Cataluña, to request two seats on the trains that were leaving for the border. In that atmosphere of improvisation and fear no one was able to help them, and mother and daughter, each with a small suitcase, began walking up the Gerona highway. When night fell they met an assault guard, who asked if they'd eaten anything. Only then did they realize they hadn't eaten a single thing all day, and the man shared with them some dry lentils he had with him: that and a miserable lemon that someone would give them the next day were all they ate until they arrived in Figueras. The first night they spent outdoors, the second they slept on the floor of a farmhouse, the third they managed to find a little space in a house in Gerona....

It has been estimated that during those days half a million Spaniards went into exile. The images of the exodus are well known: women who, in order to save something of their wardrobe, were wearing three or four dresses at once, children with heads shaven because of lice, old and disabled people walking with the help of canes and crutches, men wrapped in blankets and capes dragging huge bundles and all running in search of cover when the German and Italian bombers appeared... In the middle of that human tide were carts loaded with mattresses, furniture, bundles of clothing. The horses advanced slowly. Many of them had already come a long way, from Tarragona or further. Occasionally some car or truck crammed with people managed to get through, and a short while later Miggie and Márgara would come upon it again by the side of the road, broken down or out of petrol or hit by a bomb. The exhausted fugitives abandoned their belongings piece by piece along the way: cases, trunks, radios, sewing machines and typewriters. The cold was intense. Some camped in the hills and lit fires to get warm and to cook. When it rained hard, they hung blankets up between the trees for shelter.

Despite the hardship for those who were fleeing, in the midst of the drama there were still traces of humour. One of the men who also slept in the house in Gerona took pity on Márgara and Miggie, who were fainting with exhaustion, and offered them two places in what he called a '*carromato*.' Following his instructions, they went to the place where the *carromato* was waiting, which turned out to be a tractor pulling several broken-down cars attached to it with cables. The Robles women were allocated a dazzling red convertible. When the tractor set off, the drag of all the vehicles being towed was so great that the absurd convoy could only advance at a snail's pace. Márgara and Miggie, from their convertible, saw that even the elderly people fleeing on foot were moving faster than they were in this contraption and, feeling ridiculous, they chose to get out and walk. They arrived in Figueras when the final meeting of the Republican Parliament had already taken place in its castle. With their hunger barely alleviated by a tin of sardines, they had to set off again on 3rd February, the day of the huge bombing of the city, and Miggie remembers sleeping that night in a house occupied by some Republican soldiers who sang bitterly of their defeat.

That was how Márgara and her daughter fled from Spain, and arrived the next day in France. Before crossing the border, along with several hundred other people, they had to spend a night in a train which had stopped in the middle of a tunnel. In Cerbère, only Miggie's US passport saved them from being interned in a concentration camp. They arrived in Perpignan, a city then full of Spaniards in hiding from the raids by gendarmes who demanded to see *les papiers*. From Perpignan station they took a train to Paris, where they stayed for a few days in the hotel room of a friend who was a painter. A cheque from Johns Hopkins and another from Dos Passos saved them, according to Márgara, from being interned 'in one of those horrible concentration camps where thousands of our comrades are dying.'

During those first days in Paris, Márgara and Miggie were 'worn-out, dirty, physically and morally destroyed, wandering amid people's indifference,' and the mother's apprehension for her own situation was compounded by the lack of news of her son, making her increasingly anxious as the days passed and plunging her into deep depression: 'Awake I have hallucinations that frighten me and asleep terrible nightmares.' Later, Márgara had to stay in Chelles, a village near Paris, because the French government would not allow Spanish refugees to remain in the capital. Miggie, allowed freedom of movement thanks to her US passport, was able to get in contact with her comrades in the JSU, who gave her a job working with the *Rassemblement Mondial des Étudiants*. She moved into the Hotel Dacia on boulevard Saint-Michel, sharing a room with two girls from the *Rassemblement*, one of them Dutch and the other from Indonesia.

The *Rassemblement Mondial des Étudiants* brought together numerous student organizations from different countries, all of them anti-fascist. Its secretary was James Klugmann, a young man who had been the leader of the Cambridge Communists. Klugmann's friend, the well-known Marxist historian Eric Hobsbawm, came to work at the *Rassemblement*, and mentions in his memoirs 'little Miggy Robles, who worked so hard at the duplicator.' At her side Hobsbawm remembers a certain Pablo Azcárate, who was actually Luis Azcárate. Secretary of Agitation and Propaganda for the Barcelona JSU and a member of the Federal Union of Hispanic Students, he was the son of a well-known Republican military officer and a nephew of the Spanish Ambassador to London. One day in March, Luis Azcárate walked into the offices of the *Rassemblement*, on Arago boulevard, and offered to assist the Spanish students in the internment camps. The person in charge of that work was Miggie.

Luis' job, according to his unpublished memoirs, was to 'go and buy books, package them up and send them by post to the students.' He also wrote letters of support to the students and sent an information bulletin which they ran off themselves on the duplicator, and appealed to prominent people requesting help. One day a letter arrived from

Washington on the official letterhead of the White House. It was from Eleanor Roosevelt, who, responding to an earlier letter from Miggie, wished the Spanish students good luck. She also sent a personal greeting to her young correspondent: the first lady of the United States still remembered the awkward situation she'd put her in on that occasion in August of the previous year.

Luis and Miggie, seventeen and fifteen years old respectively, soon fell in love. They went for walks in the Jardin du Luxembourg, kissed on the stairs of the Saint-Michel metro station... The outbreak of the Second World War abruptly interrupted this idyll. On 1st September the German army invaded Poland, and France and England were forced to declare war on the Axis powers. The Maginot line, which would turn out to be so weak, should have protected the French from the anticipated German invasion. In the middle of October, Luis, just back from a trip, rushed to the Hotel Dacia to see Miggie. On one of the nearby boulevards, dark because of the blackout, he ran straight into her and her mother. He introduced himself with a voice choked with shyness, and Márgara burst out laughing and kissed him on the cheek. Then the two youngsters went for a walk beside the Seine. Miggie told him then of their plan to leave France.

Mother and daughter began their umpteenth escape at the end of that month. Back in April Márgara had looked into the possibility of travelling to the United States, and in the summer had bought tickets for a transatlantic ship belonging to a German company that was due to embark on 3rd September. The voyage was cancelled because of the outbreak of war. When he heard of this, Coindreau wrote to

Lancaster: 'And now they will have to go through another war! I never heard of such bad luck. I am very much afraid they will be sent to a concentration camp.'

In fact, by October their hardships were about to come to an end. From Paris Márgara and Miggie travelled to Bordeaux, and there, not without a certain amount of suspense (Márgara left their tickets and documents in a taxi, but they managed to recover them), they embarked on a Ward Line ship for New York. Márgara was absolutely devastated: her husband accused of treason and shot, her son locked up in prison and condemned to death, her own country closed to her for who knew how long, she and her daughter forced into constant flight. As they boarded the ship that was to take them back to North America, Márgara remembered with tears in her eyes the last time she had crossed the same ocean: to think they had just been planning to spend the summer holidays in Spain.

On 12th November they arrived in Baltimore, where for a couple of weeks they were the guests of Professor Henry Carrington Lancaster. In Baltimore Márgara was at least able to collect on her husband's insurance policy and the royalties from his last book, now that his death by execution had finally been officially confirmed. The death certificate had arrived at Johns Hopkins University in August along with a letter from Márgara which said: 'Please find enclosed this document, proof of our misfortune, which the former government of the Republic has finally been kind enough to give me.' After all that time, it appears Juan Negrín had signed the document at Marcelino Pascua's insistence. With the money, Márgara and her daughter settled their debts in the United States and bought two tickets on a Greyhound bus to Mexico City at the end of November 1939. They became two more of the thirty thousand Spanish Republicans that President Lázaro Cárdenas took in.

Living conditions in the Spanish jails did not change when the Civil War ended. Coco's situation did, however. On 23rd October 1939, his death sentence was commuted to one of thirty years imprisonment. We can imagine how he would have been notified of the commutation from Ramón Rufat's description of the way it happened to him. 'The simple and unshowy way a person can pass from death to life has to be seen to be believed! They call you into a tiny room, not even the judges' room, and there a soldier or at most a corporal reads a paper to you that he said was a decree, he writes a couple of lines for you in his good or bad handwriting and makes you sign it to prove that he had communicated it to you and that you were informed.'

It seems that the revision of Coco's sentence was due to the personal intervention of an influential man in the new regime, Juan Contreras y López de Ayala, marquis of Lozoya, from Segovia. He had been a good friend of José Robles, and during the Franco years became a renowned art historian. The intercession of the US Embassy also may have had an influence, and documents show that Johns Hopkins had continued to press them to help Coco. In a letter from August 1940, Ambassador Alexander Weddell asked Lancaster to consider 'the difficulty of doing anything except in an informal and unofficial way for anyone not an American citizen,' and assured him that his own wife had 'attempted to minister to his physical wants by sending food and clothing from time to time.' A few months earlier, Coco himself had written to Lancaster to congratulate him for an act of homage his old students were going to pay him, and also to thank him for the 'valuable help' he'd given his family. Another of his Baltimore benefactors was Esther Crooks, who in May had written to the State Department to ask them to try to get him freed and had promised to take care of him: 'I shall be glad to have him live with me and be responsible for all his expenses. I should also be willing to legally adopt the boy, if that would be of any benefit.' Dos Passos and Katy also offered to adopt him. Coco, who heard about this in a letter from his mother received at the beginning of July, was flattered, and immediately wrote to Dos and his wife to express his gratitude. But the initiative was not likely to have any effect, and, in his reply to Márgara, Coco predicted: 'Very little will be achieved through such channels.'

From this time on, information on Coco's itinerary through Franco's penitentiaries is vague, but on 26th March 1943, when the *Commissión de Examen de Penas* confirmed his sentence, he was still in the Torrero prison. In deplorable conditions, he had survived the terror of the '*sacas*' (when gangs of fascists raided the prisons at night, took men out and shot them), the overcrowding, the beatings, the lack of hygiene, the malnutrition. He had also survived the not inconsiderable risk of illness. According to Ramón Rufat, the widespread scabies of the first months in the Zaragoza prison were followed by boils, anthrax, jaundice, tuberculosis, constant vitamin deficiencies and, finally, a plague of 'green lice' or typhus exanthema, which kept all the prisoners subject to quarantine: 'No one came into or went out of the prison during those forty days. Only corpses left.'

Of Coco's activities inside the prison we know only what little he wanted to (or could) tell in his letters: that he gave lessons to other inmates ('I've grown to like teaching'), that he devoted his free time to study and reading ('I've just started to read Seneca'). According to some sources, the receipt of packages was restricted until 1942. That must have been when he began to receive occasional visits from a young woman who took an interest in him and brought him food: she was what was known as a '*madrina*' or benefactor. Those visits were the only thing that gave him any happiness during the time he spent in the Zaragoza prison. A necessarily platonic relationship between Coco and the girl grew, and they undoubtedly made plans for when he was freed. But a long time was to pass before then, and meanwhile, to Coco's despair, the girl contracted tuberculosis and died.

Before regaining his liberty, Coco still had to spend time in two more jails. On 25th August 1943, he was shackled again and driven to the station, where he was put on a train to Burgos. He must have been in the Central Prison of that city until at least 4th January of the following year, when the thirty years imprisonment in conditions of maximum security were commuted to twenty years of imprisonment, which (after a catechism exam, required for the mandatory chaplain's report) would open the doors to conditional liberty. He was notified of this on 16th April, but by then he was no longer in the Burgos prison but in that of Lora del Río, in the province of Seville, the last stage of his long penitentiary journey.

In all this time, the only family member in a position to do so did not intercede for Coco. His Uncle Ramón had been promoted to the rank of lieutenant colonel for mentions in dispatches, and his numerous decorations earned during the Civil War were added to by those earned, between April 1942 and April 1943, fighting on the Russian front with the *División Azul*. One who did help was his Aunt Mari, who, at least from the time Coco was interned in the Burgos prison, visited him occasionally and took him food parcels.

María Robles Pazos, like Ramón and their two sisters, was part of the Spain of the victors, but her charitable and generous nature led her to forget political differences and offer her protection. That protection began towards the middle of the five-year period Coco spent in the Torrero penitentiary. She first requested a pardon in October 1942 on the grounds that her nephew had not held 'the least rank in the red army,' as well as his 'true vocation for study' (Coco had attended a school for gifted children), and the unanimous respect and admiration he had earned among his classmates and teachers in the 'Catholic Maryland of the United States.' In that same document María Robles referred to 'his circumstantially forced and resolutely tragic affiliation to the enemy cause,' which could be interpreted as a recognition of Coco's past membership in the Communist Party, a militancy with little enthusiasm and merely by chance, if we are to believe the phrasing of the request.

It was also his Aunt Mari who, in April 1944, took him into her flat at number 100 Calle de Alcalá in Madrid. Coco was then a physically and morally battered, if not broken, man and looked much older than his twenty-four years. In

the oppressive atmosphere of the initial postwar period, Coco thought only of getting out of Spain, a country in which fate had dealt him the most invidious experiences. That was no easy task, however. He applied to Johns Hopkins University for a scholarship. With references from John Dos Passos and Elliot Paul, Johns Hopkins had offered him a similar unsolicited scholarship in 1940, when Coco was still imprisoned in the Zaragoza penitentiary, which made him think his application would receive a favourable reception. And indeed it did. With surprising speed the scholarship was granted in May. But since he had only been granted conditional liberty, he was refused a passport and had to turn it down.

During the summer of 1944, accompanied by his benefactor, he spent some time recovering in Galicia, in a house belonging to the Robles family in Villajuán, beside the Ría de Arosa in Pontevedra. On 30th June he wrote to Dos Passos to tell him that he had 'returned to an almost normal life': he was swimming, fishing, reading. However, Coco had not fulfilled his military obligations to Franco's Spain, and very soon afterwards had to join the army. From the photos he sent to his mother and sister we can deduce that he carried out his military service somewhere near the Pyrenees. What is known is that he was not discharged until the end of November 1945.

A couple of weeks before this date he had written to the US Embassy offering to work in the Embassy itself or in the Casa Americana. Coco did not waver in his determination to leave Spain as soon as possible, and in that letter he also requested help in obtaining the authorization to leave the country. However, being a former Communist was a serious obstacle to his aspirations. In February 1946 he again requested a pardon, which was denied him on 13th June. This time, too, his past activism counted against him. On one of the acknowledgements accompanying the application requesting the pardon, someone wrote the following words in pencil: 'Communist. He has to recant.'

In the library of the Casa Americana Coco read some of the latest American literature, including Dos Passos' most recent works, to whom he wrote with his impressions and to tell him about the Spanish situation: 'Living in Spain during these past years has been (and goes on being) like living on another planet.' He had begun to look for work, while living in his Aunt Mari's flat once again. All he could manage to find, however, were a few students for private English lessons. One of his students, a daughter of one of Márgara's cousins, was called Dolores Cebrián, Loli. She and Coco fell in love and made plans to marry. But his new civil status did not alter his plans to leave Spain. In the autumn of 1947, barely a week after the ceremony, he travelled to the Basque Country along with his friend Ricardo Ortiz and managed to get to France on a fishing boat. On 14th November, an anxious Márgara wrote to Dos Passos: 'I am like an idiot with the idea that I might soon see him again after almost nine years.' Coco's difficulties in getting a ticket prolonged the wait, and it wasn't until the end of January that he wrote to Dos Passos to tell him that on the seventh of that month he had finally been reunited with Márgara and Miggie at their home at number 300 Calle Lerma, not far from the Paseo de la Reforma in the Mexican capital. Some time later his wife joined him there. Coco would live in Mexico until his death in 1990, and only

in his final years, once Franco was dead, would he again step on Spanish soil.

Between 1942 and 1944, Miggie had studied for a degree in Romance Languages at Swarthmore College in Pennsylvania, thanks to a small scholarship and, especially, to financial help from her godfather, Maurice Coindreau, who was still teaching at Princeton University. As a tribute to Coindreau, the second of her four children, who in time would become a writer, is named after him. Miggie married Anselmo Ortiz in 1945. Anselmo also came from a family of Spanish exiles, and remarkably, his brother Ricardo, who escaped from Spain with Coco, a few years later married Nora Nin, one of Andreu Nin's two daughters. By one of those strange twists of fate, two of the most important victims of Stalinism in Spain ended up posthumously related by marriage.

There are a number of photos from that period of Márgara's and Miggie's lives. In one of them, taken in 1943 during a countryside walk, mother and daughter appear with their arms around each other with the Iztlaccíhuatl volcano in the background. More than half a century later, that photo would inspire a moving text by Miggie's son, the writer Mauricio Ortiz, who evoked Márgara in this way: 'Grandmother had once had all in love, our young grandfather murdered years before, and the rest of her days spent with nothing to occupy her but sewing memories into colourful quilts.' By the time they were reunited with Coco, Márgara had gone back to working as a translator, which she'd given up in 1932. Even today her Spanish version of *Rocinante vuelve al camino* is reissued from time to time, and the Mexican publisher Fondo de Cultura Económica, for which she translated nine books, still has several of them in their catalogue. Márgara (who now, in homage to her husband, signed her publications Margarita Villegas de Robles) lived until 1983, but her last translation, a non-fiction book on archaeology in Crete, was published in 1965.

What has never been out of print is the Spanish version José Robles Pazos produced of *Manhattan Transfer* for Cenit. Until the 1970s it always appeared with his name and both surnames. In the editions from the early eighties, the printer's gremlins mysteriously deprived him of his second surname. Those same gremlins, however, had a much worse fate in reserve. In new editions after 1984 José Robles was named as José Robles Piquer, and still appears that way in some of the most recent editions. It's hard to imagine a more sinister little joke: as if by magic, the most defeated of the defeated has been incorporated into one of the most illustrious lineages of Franco's victorious regime.

# APPENDIX

The earliest mention of Hemingway in the Spanish literary press came in the glowing review by José Robles of *Fiesta* in the June 1927 issue of *La Gaceta Literaria*, and the first of his works to be translated into Spanish was 'The Killers,' one of the best-known short stories of his early period. 'Los matones' was included in a volume called *10 novelistas americanos* that Zeus published in 1932. Zeus, like Cenit, was one of the distinguished leftist publishers of the time. So it is not surprising that the editor in charge of the selection, Julián Gorkin, should have declared in the preface his aim of bringing to the reading public's attention 'independent, socially inspired literature, whose representatives were having to wage a titanic struggle against the plutocrats and their money, prohibitionist hypocrites and Bible-readers.' The list of authors included the most conspicuous of American writers considered close to socialism, among them John Dos Passos, whose work was already known in Spain thanks to the translations by José Robles and Márgara Villegas.

The anthologist, who would not have known him personally at the time, described Dos Passos as 'indisputably, one of the most modern novelists who exist.' Though they had not yet met, they would at some point develop a friendly relationship which would last for several decades, as suggested by the text Dos Passos wrote as a prologue to Gorkin's novel *Death in Hand*, published in Argentina in 1956. Could it be that their first meeting took place in April 1937, when the American visited the Barcelona offices of the POUM, where Gorkin was a member of the Executive Committee? This is simply conjecture but does not seem implausible.

By the time the anthology appeared, Julián Gorkin, whose real name was Julián Gómez García, had published a couple of pieces of political theatre (the designation is his), a novel called *Days of Bohemia* and a few translations. More distinguished, however, as a left-wing activist than as a literary man, it is no accident that his autobiography bears the title *Professional Revolutionary*. Gorkin, an exile in Paris since 1921, travelled to Moscow in March 1925, and Andreu Nin, senior secretary at the Profintern, warned him of the atmosphere of intrigue and suspicion that had become widespread since Lenin's death and the resulting power struggles. Soon afterward, Gorkin found out that the letters he had been sending to his wife, 'full of reservations with respect to the USSR and the International,' had been intercepted and were in the hands of the GPU. Before leaving the country he paid a visit to the mausoleum where Lenin's embalmed corpse was on display and held an imaginary dialogue with him: 'I have glimpsed everywhere the terrifying silhouette of the monster: the growing bureaucracy, corruption, avid and manipulative ambition, venomous intrigue, the mentality and methods of a police state.... Has all this emerged since your death or should we look to Bolshevism itself for the root of the evil?'

His rupture with the Comintern did not take place until 1929. To provoke his exclusion he had only to translate the essay *The Disfigured Revolution*, in which Trotsky condemned the bureaucratization of the Soviet regime. After that,

Gorkin earned his living working from Paris with the main Spanish left-wing publishers, and in September 1935 he participated in the founding of the POUM, product of the fusion of Joaquín Maurín's *Bloque Obrero y Campesino* and Andreu Nin's *Izquierda Comunista Española*. The new party, though routinely branded as Trotskyist, had actually been created against the advice of Trotsky, who, in vain, had given instructions to his Spanish supporters to join the PSOE. Trotskyists or not, Julián Gorkin and his comrades in the POUM would soon suffer a persecution similar to the one the USSR had already unleashed against Stalin's opponents.

Three years later, in 1938, a book appeared called *Espionage in Spain,* which collected and presented as irrefutable truth the fake evidence that implicated the POUM leaders in a Falangist conspiracy. Its translators, Lucienne and Arturo Perucho, may be unfamiliar, but its supposed author, an improbable Max Rieger, is completely unknown. The same cannot be said for the author of the prologue, the Catholic and Communist poet José Bergamín. He must have suspected the contents of the book were nothing but vile slurs yet, in spite of everything, he quite unashamedly wrote that 'the facts here related, extreme though they may be, demonstrate the real nature of a counterrevolutionary and fascist effort.' At a moment like that and under such circumstances, to declare, as Bergamín did, that Nin's party was not 'an organization cohabiting with the enemy, but the enemy itself' meant legitimizing the brutal repression against the POUM. He even makes use of the occasion to attack the 'anguished' French intellectuals who had sent a telegram demanding the defendants be given due procedural rights. 'Procedural rights?' a sarcastic Bergamín wonders, 'how can they ask such a thing of a government which practically takes them to extremes, and, as this case in particular is demonstrating, even to an exaggerated degree?'

In *Following the Footsteps of a Ghost*, Professor Gonzalo Penalva says that Bergamín, then president of the Alliance of Anti-fascist Intellectuals, accepted the invitation to write a prologue for the book because Juan Negrín asked him to and because he sincerely believed in the veracity of the accusations. This second reason seems more than dubious, given that Bergamín, though a recent convert to Communism, knew Nin, Gorkin and company's irreproachable revolutionary trajectory, and that someone like him must surely have harboured some reservations about the ludicrous theory of a conspiracy of Falangists and members of the POUM. But any such reservations were never expressed and, years later, instead of recognizing the error of having written that prologue, he still claimed 'categorically, in the same circumstances, he would write it a hundred times.' Gonzalo Penalva is not mistaken when, compared to the cowardice of the disguised author of the book, he praises Bergamín for at least having the courage to sign the prologue with his real name. Who hid behind the pseudonym Max Rieger? From an April 1939 report by Stepanov, delegate of the Comintern in Spain, we know that it was a collective work and that Stepanov himself had a hand in its preparation. In *Dear Comrades* Antonio Elorza and Marta Bizcarrondo suggest that it might also have included contributions by the French Communist writer Georges Soria, author of articles in *International Corres-*

*pondence*, which coincide in many instances with the text of *Espionage in Spain*. Nevertheless, according to numerous never-denied testimonies, the principal coordinator of the book was an old friend of José Robles, professor of Roman Law and translator Wenceslao Roces.

Writing texts for other people must have been one of his habitual activities for, according to the former chief of the Fifth Regiment Enrique Castro Delgado, Roces was the author of some of the speeches of the then minister of Public Education, the Communist Jesús Hernández. At that time Roces was an undersecretary of the ministry; if we are to believe Antonio Machado, education in Spain owed as much to the undersecretary and minister 'as to a century's worth of their predecessors.' Wenceslao Roces, a short timid-looking Asturian, produced some of the most widely used Spanish translations of Hegel and of Marx and, until then, the most prominent event of his biography was the violent attack in the summer of 1933 at the Madrid Offices of the Association of Friends of the USSR, of which he was a victim, by members of the protofascist *Juntas de Ofensiva Nacional Sindicalista* led by Ramiro Ledesma Ramos.

His profile was that of a grey and uncharismatic man, who always put himself in the shadow of more dazzling figures. For the duration of the Writers' Congress in Defense of Culture, organized by the Alliance of Anti-fascist Intellectuals in close collaboration with the Ministry of Education (that is, by Bergamín and Roces, but also by the omnipresent Koltsov), one of those figures was Bergamín. 'Thin, dark-skinned, bird-like,' as Malcolm Cowley described him, he dictated the official line of the Congress and hogged the limelight with his public condemnation of two books in which his former friend André Gide criticized the atmosphere of persecution and lack of liberty he had perceived on his last trip to the USSR. Meanwhile, Roces, a disciplinarian and lover of hierarchy, held power in the shadows and was, according to Arturo Serrano Plaja, the one who made appointments and accepted or refused initiatives.

Wenceslao Roces did not always acquit himself very gracefully with the participating writers. The most often repeated episode is his censoring of Luis Cernuda's poem 'To A Dead Poet,' with which Cernuda wished to pay homage to Federico García Lorca in the journal *Hora de España* and from which Roces obliged him to delete a stanza that alluded explicitly to Lorca's homosexuality. Less well known is the story revealed by the then wife of Octavio Paz in *Memories of Spain, 1937*. According to Elena Garro, who knew only that Roces 'was a Party member and that he spoke Russian,' the poet León Felipe felt persecuted by him, telling her that he had thrown him out of his assigned living quarters in Valencia and later threatened his life. 'He wants to kill me, the swine...! Kill me...!' León Felipe repeated, now out of Spain and somewhat calmer.

Whether or not he wanted to kill him is something we cannot know. We do know that in the fifth issue of *Hora de España* León Felipe published a long fragment of his poem 'La insignia,' and that Roces submitted him to a tough interrogation about the verses that denounced cases of theft committed by some Republicans. We also know that, in July, Wenceslao Roces opted for the dissolution of the 'House of the Wise,' where Dos Passos had stayed in April. As noted earlier, the Casa de la Cultura served as a residence for eminent Republican scientists, artists and writers. One of these was León Felipe. Another, the doctor Gonzalo R. Lafora, who had been the director of the Institute of Psychiatry and who, in an article published in the daily *Fragua Social*, the newspaper of the CNT local, protested energetically against this measure. In this article, Lafora attributed the closure to 'the lamentable actions of señor Roces,' whom he criticized for his methods 'of personal revenge, political oppression and taunts against those who did not meekly follow his instructions, paying no attention to or respecting names nor long histories of democratic conduct.' The Communist press counterattacked, saying that the Casa de la Cultura was not being closed but transformed into a centre of work and investigation; among Roces' defenders were some of the residents and also Antonio Machado, who, in spite of being gravely ill, agreed to chair the board of the new institution.

Another person who felt affronted by Roces' authoritarian ways was Francisco Ayala, who, without being consulted, was chosen by him to become the dean of the Faculty of Law at the University of Madrid. Fearful that his appointment could expose his family to reprisals in Burgos, Ayala called 'the imbecile' Roces, who threatened to send him to the front and ordered that, if he had to contact him, 'he should do so through the appropriate hierarchical channels.' The telephone conversation was brought to an abrupt conclusion by Ayala. 'Look, Roces – I said – go to hell!' The truth is, apart from the occasional formal and forced expression of support, comments on the undersecretary of Public Education encourage little sympathy, and some critics had stronger reasons than Ayala to detest him. Although he offers no proof, Julián Gorkin claims in *Moscow Trials in Barcelona* that it was Wenceslao Roces, who, together with a nephew of General Miaja and several of Alexander Orlov's right-hand men, falsified the plan that would serve to implicate the POUM leaders in the espionage plot of the Falangist agent Golfín.

In his prologue, Bergamín assures readers that *Espionage in Spain* 'offers, besides the precise documentation, evidence in itself, the exact record of some facts.' The reality, however, seems to be quite the opposite: what was presented there was faked documentation that aspired to prove a delirious and completely groundless plot. The book, published in Spain by Ediciones Unidad, appeared in other countries from publishers also controlled by the Comintern. Rushed into print for the occasion, the book, which was also used for propaganda, was used as evidence against the POUM men during the interrogations they were subjected to by the Tribunal of Espionage and High Treason. The strangest thing is that, when witnesses were called to testify for the defence, the former Ambassador to Paris, Luis Araquistáin, also offered a book as evidence. It was not a book that had been thrown together in haste to refute the allegations of *Espionage in Spain*. It was a book by Trotsky called *My Adventures in Spain*, which had been published in 1929, in Andreu Nin's translation, by España Books, which was then run by Araquistáin, Juan Negrín and Julio Álvarez del Vayo. The latter (Araquistáin's brother-in-law, incidentally) was also the author of the prologue, a biographical sketch of Trotsky full of passionate praise. The question facing the tribunal posed by the book Araquistáin held in his hand could not have been more blunt: with Negrín being president of the Council of Ministers and Álvarez del Vayo Minister of State, how could those in government accuse anyone of being Trotskyists and declare themselves to be anti-Trotskyists? A similar question could be asked of the anti-Trotskyist Roces if, instead of remaining in the shadows, he had appeared in court. For *My Adventures in Spain* is not the only book by Trotsky that had been published in Spanish. Of the four titles of his that appear in the Cenit catalogue, two were translated by Nin and one by Gorkin. The translator of the fourth was none other than Wenceslao Roces. Is there room for any more contradictions?

The Executive Committee of the POUM had met on the morning of 16th June 1937 in their office in the Palacio de la Virreina, then called the Instituto Joaquín Maurín. After discussing the question of whether or not Gorkin, who was editor of *La Batalla*, should attend the trial against the newspaper, they moved to another of the party's buildings, which was also located on the Ramblas. That was where two plain-clothes agents arrested Nin. In the afternoon, the remaining members of the Committee received several pieces of alarming news: their homes had been stormed, their wives detained, the party's premises occupied. Around eleven o'clock that night they were themselves arrested by assault guards. Gorkin and his comrades were sent to different cells in Valencia and Madrid until, now aware of the accusation of espionage and high treason hanging over them, they were returned to Barcelona, where they were interned in a convent on Calle Deu i Mata converted into a state prison. By the beginning of June of the following year, the special judge in charge of trying the case had finished his work. The hearing took place in the middle of October and lasted eleven days, and the tribunal took another ten to pass sentence, which absolved Gorkin and his comrades of the principal accusations but considered them guilty of the secondary charges.

Among the members of the Executive Committee who spent time in jails and *chekas* was Juan Andrade, 'tall and bony, long-faced and toothless, a Madrid man frugal with word and gestures,' according to Gorkin's description. Oddly, John Dos Passos had been involved in his move towards Communism, although indirectly. The story goes back to 1919 and the arrival in Spain of the American Charles Phillips, one of the two emissaries the Communist International had sent with the mission of creating a Spanish section of the organization. Phillips spoke Spanish with a Mexican accent and called himself Jesús Ramírez. The first contacts he'd established in Madrid had come to nothing when he dropped into the library of the Ateneo and met a fair-haired young man wearing glasses and reading books in English. The young man was Dos Passos, who introduced him to two Spanish socialists who were reading at the next desks. One of them was Fernando de los Ríos, the minister whose 1933 meeting in Santander Dos Passos would write up in 'The Republic of Honest Men'; the other was the city councillor Mariano García Cortés. Through him, Phillips established relations with those who would become his principal supporters in the foundation of the

Spanish Communist Party (PCE), among them, the young Juan Andrade.

After his encounter with the American Communist, Andrade's biography is that of an archetypal revolutionary. Having co-founded the PCE in 1920, Andrade gave up all his positions within the party seven years later due to the Soviet revolution's Stalinist change of direction. As in the case of Gorkin and so many others, his conversion can be explained, as François Furet suggests, in religious terms: 'the believer's enthusiasm would be replaced by the critical eye, and the very events that had illuminated an entire existence would lose their source of light.' In 1930, Andrade was involved in writing the constitution of the Spanish Communist Left (ICE), one of the two parties that in 1935 united to form the POUM. An autodidact educated in the Ateneo's library, Andrade edited several Marxist publications, and his enormous capacity for work made him an indispensable element in many of the revolutionary undertakings of the time. Left-wing publishing houses such as Oriente or Hoy would have had difficulty surviving without him, and the same could be said of Cenit, which he founded along with Graco Marsá and Rafael Giménez Siles.

Three of the most relevant figures of the POUM, therefore, had been closely linked to Cenit: Andrade as founder, Nin as translator of seven works, Gorkin as translator of five. Of course, they are not the only characters of this story who worked for the publisher. After all, it was Cenit that published José Robles' and Márgara Villegas' translations of books by John Dos Passos and other authors. Ramón J. Sender also published four books with Cenit. And as well as

Trotsky, Wenceslao Roces translated Marx, Engels, Zweig, Remarque and another seven authors for Cenit.

The history of Cenit, along with that of other leftist publishing houses of the day, has been studied by Gonzalo Santonja in *The Republic of Books*. It all started at the end of Primo de Rivera's dictatorship. There was a pre-publication censorship regime in force at the time from which books more than two hundred pages long were exempt. To get around this censorship, several young revolutionaries connected to the magazine *Post-Guerra* decided to publish books and founded Ediciones Oriente. The most optimistic forecasts predicted a precarious survival, if not closure, and the unexpected success of the first eight titles revealed a potential readership unknown up till then. Those eight titles included one by Malraux, another by Trotsky, another by Juan Andrade. He and Rafael Giménez Siles, former members of the *Post-Guerra* group, decided to do without their other associates and mine the possibilities of the recently discovered seam on their own account. For the new editorial project they also relied on Graco Marsá, whom Giménez Siles had met in February 1928 in Madrid's Model Prison, where they were both serving sentences for anti-monarchist activities. Marsá was a republican lawyer of radical tendencies who had recently inherited from his grandfather the not inconsiderable sum of thirty thousand pesetas. The conversations leading to the constitution of the company took place in the prison itself, where Andrade frequently visited them, and by December of the same year *The Religious Problem in Mexico*, Cenit's first book, was already in bookshops.

The following year would see the publication of *A Spanish Notary in Russia*, by Diego Hidalgo, who would later be elected to represent Badajoz and reach the position of War Minister in the government of Lerroux. In the book itself Hidalgo tells how, in September 1928, while taking interminable steps to obtain a visa to enter the USSR, he met Julián Gorkin in Paris and how, in Moscow, he also met Álvarez del Vayo, then still a journalist, who had been invited to the celebrations of Tolstoy's centenary and was received with familiarity in the most diverse official offices. Hidalgo's book, of which they sold out four print runs before 1936, was one of Cenit's biggest successes, but the main economic support its author provided to the publishing house consisted in assuring its liquidity with his personal fortune.

Hidalgo's was not, and far from it, the only book Cenit published about the USSR. In a catalogue dominated by works that celebrate the achievements of the revolution, the presence of *Russia Unveiled*, by Panaït Istrati, stands out. The book, translated under a pseudonym by Julián Gorkin and published in 1930, just a year after its appearance in France, is considered to be the first by a Communist disillusioned by what he saw in the Soviet Union, and has been defined by Furet as an antidote 'to the fairy tales of the Soviet journey that were just then catching on.' *Russia Unveiled* caused the rupture between Giménez Siles and Andrade. The former, although never a member of any party, was much closer to Communist orthodoxy than the second, a declared Trotskyist, who left Cenit to carry on his own editorial career with Ediciones Hoy. Graco Marsá soon followed in Andrade's footsteps, and in the summer of 1930 left Giménez Siles to found Zeus.

Cenit would carry on until a month before the Civil War. In those eight years, Giménez Siles published more than two hundred books distributed in twenty-five series, including: The Proletarian Novel, New Novelists and Social Criticism, the Karl Marx Library, Cenit Stories for Children... In this last collection, incidentally, they published in 1931 a book by L. Panteleiew called *The Clock or The Adventures of Petika,* dedicated by the editor to Coco and Miggie Robles. Giménez Siles was one of the great Spanish publishers of those years. As well as his activity at the head of Cenit he was also a promoter of various magazines and the driving force behind initiatives such as the Madrid Book Fair or the mobile bookshops, which brought culture to the most far-flung corners of the peninsula. Giménez Siles' organizational capacity is almost legendary. The case of Cenit shows this clearly, for it was he, almost single-handedly, who kept the publishing house going after Andrade and Marsá's early resignations.

Although, in fact, during some of those years he was not entirely alone. At his side was Wenceslao Roces, with whom he'd worked on the magazine *The Student* just as Andrade had at *Post-Guerra*. A simple glance at the publisher's catalogue confirms that Roces as well as Gorkin and Nin worked for Cenit from the start. The intense contribution of the latter two was cut short, however, quite early: Gorkin's last translation was published in 1931 and Nin's in 1932. It is quite likely that this break had something to do with the rupture between Giménez Siles and Andrade, one of whose works was announced as forthcoming and never even published. Andrade soon founded, together with the other two, the POUM, and his departure from Cenit coincided with a significant increase in Roces' influence. While not giving up others within the publishing house, he began to edit the recently created Karl Marx Library series and, if Giménez Siles had to do without his contribution temporarily during the so-called *bienio negro* – the two black years – it was not through any choice of his own. At the end of 1934, as a consequence of the repression unleashed after the Asturian miners' uprising, Wenceslao Roces was arrested and imprisoned and, after obtaining, thanks to Diego Hidalgo, provisional liberty, hurried to seek refuge in Russia.

In a 1929 interview quoted by Santonja, Giménez Siles announced the publication of *The Disfigured Revolution*, 'a study that, due to the grave accusations it contained against the figures currently in charge of Russian communism, Trotsky could not publish or even send to his friends outside of Russia until he himself was out of the territory of the USSR.' The book was in fact published but was deleted from the editorial catalogue a short time later, and the same fate befell *Russia Unveiled*. Cenit's obedience to Soviet orthodoxy grew to the point that in February 1936 the Comintern chose it as the publisher that should channel its propaganda in Spain: for this purpose, the governing body of the Comintern allocated the considerable sum of fifty thousand pesetas, which Cenit would share with a newly created cultural magazine. Santonja says that Andrade's departure 'does not admit the simplistic explanation of characterizing Siles or Roces, or both, with clichéd appraisals from the anti-Stalinist handbook.' What he does not say is that Andrade's fall and Roces' rise reflected in the heart of the publishing house the same rupture that was taking place within the Spanish revolutionary left and which, in turn, was a reflection of the policy of crushing dissidence that was being rolled out in the USSR: a rupture, in any case, that would continue to grow and would leave some on the side of the persecuted and others on that of the persecutors. The history of Cenit can thus be seen as a warning and a metaphor of that other persecution, vaster and bloodier, that would soon be unleashed as a consequence of the Civil War.

The most illustrious victim of that persecution was, of course, Andreu Nin. It would be hard to find a more complete description than that by Josep Pla, who met Nin in Moscow in mid-1925, 'a man of average height, stocky but not obese, strong, well-built, with well-defined features: curved nose, small mouth and ears, even, admirable white teeth, big eyes of the same dark brown colour as his hair, pale, almost greyish skin occasionally tinged with light pink blotches, sharp chin and cheeks. With somewhat short but well muscled legs, he planted his feet on the floor with considerable stability...' The friendship between the two men was forged in the six weeks the Catalan writer spent in the Soviet Union as special correspondent for the newspaper *La Publicitat*. Thirty-three years after that trip, Pla would write a profile of Nin in a second series of his *Homenots*, and his words transmit very little sympathy for a figure he'd elsewhere described as an 'unfortunate and unforgettable friend.' Taking for granted his merits as translator into Catalan of Tolstoy and Dostoyevsky, and recognizing some of his political virtues, Pla presents Andreu Nin as a dogmatic and resentful man, someone whose experience of the Soviet system had turned him into 'a cold, glacial, egotistic, ambitious agitator.'

Nin was the Spaniard who reached the position of most power in the USSR. When Pla met him, as well as secretary adjunct of the Profintern, he was also a representative in the Soviet of Moscow. Wilebaldo Solano, who during the war would be general secretary of the youth wing of the POUM, has emphasized the love Nin felt for the Russian people, for 'their spontaneity, humanity, naturalness and revolutionary enthusiasm.' In Moscow he married a young local activist, and only Stalin's reprisals against those like him who had joined the opposition group led by Trotsky drove him to change his place of residence. Removed from his posts and expelled from the Communist Party at the end of 1928, banned from any political activity and watched all through 1929, he managed to escape from the USSR in the summer of 1930, and with him his two daughters, Ira and Nora, and his wife, Olga Taeeva, who obtained authorization to leave the country after writing a letter in which she threatened to take her own life.

His later political evolution in Spain has been studied by Francesc Bonamusa in *Andreu Nin and the Communist Movement in Spain*: his abundant and eventually tense epistolary relationship with Trotsky, his frequent differences with Joaquín Maurín, the founding of the POUM after the fusion of the Spanish Communist Left with the Workers' and Peasants' Block.... During those years, his activity as a translator of Russian literature into Spanish and Catalan constituted his principal (and at the time, only) source of income: no fewer than twenty-six published translations, to which should be added one or two unpublished, such as a series of writings by Vladimir Antonov Ovseenko on the Red Army which seems to have been lost near the end of 1936.

Once the war began, Antonov Ovseenko, member of the Bolshevik old guard and alleged leader of the assault on the Winter Palace in 1917, was named the USSR's consul general to Barcelona, where he arrived on 1st October 1936. By then, the absence of Maurín, trapped by the war in Galicia, had made Nin the indisputable leader of the POUM, and as representative of this party he occupied the Commission of Justice and Law in the recently formed government of the *Generalitat*. Nin and Antonov Ovseenko had been friends in Moscow and had even collaborated on the same platform in opposition to Stalin. Now, however, Antonov Ovseenko was far from any Trotskyist whims, and the first encounter between the two (when, as the only member of the government who spoke Russian, it fell to Nin to deliver the welcome speech) must have been tense and formal: in fact, Antonov Ovseenko pretended not to recognize Nin. Two weeks later they coincided at another official function, and again on that occasion Nin had to serve as interpreter. Both of them knew, however, that they were on opposite sides: Antonov Ovseenko had made it clear that the possible increase in Soviet aid to Catalonia was conditional on the expulsion of the supposed Trotskyists from the government of the *Generalitat*. His pressure soon brought about the desired result, and Nin was dropped from the ministry in mid-December, after barely two and a half months in the post.

The Soviet consul was also one of the driving forces behind the repression of the POUM, but the most visible instigators were the Spanish and Catalan sections of the Comintern (that is, the PCE and the PSUC) through their official organs. Representatives in Spain of the policies of Hitler, Trotskyists under the orders of international fascism, fifth-columnists financed by the secret services of Germany and Italy...: that was how POUM members were described in those publications. Caricatures also proliferated, representing the POUM removing a hammer and sickle mask to reveal a horrific face etched with a swastika or showing Nin and Franco in a friendly handshake, and Nin himself denounced the publications of the PSUC for saying that he 'had never had to work because he'd always received a salary from Hitler.'

The campaign against the so-called Spanish Trotskyists began not long after the first of the Moscow trials, in August 1936, and coincided with the second, in January 1937. The new rhetoric of the Communist media restricted itself to reproducing the terms of the Stalinist accusations against the Bolshevik old guard, accusations they considered proved the existence of Trotskyist plots intended to bring down the Soviet regime with the support of foreign fascist governments. In his meetings, Andreu Nin responded by saying that they could eliminate them from the government but, to eliminate them from political life, 'they would have to kill all the POUM members.' However, neither he nor his comrades took seriously the possibility that the persecution would reach in Spain the blood-spattered levels it had in Russia. María Teresa García Banús, Juan Andrade's wife, remembered many years later the American Louis Fischer advising them to be careful, 'for he was sure the USSR aimed to exterminate the POUM, a warning that seemed to us incredible at the time and to which we paid scant attention.'

Andreu Nin also paid little attention to a similar warning he received at the end of April from Liston Oak in the presence of John Dos Passos. And, nevertheless, the worst of the repression was just about to arrive. The afternoon of 3rd May, only a day after Oak and Dos Passos left Spain, a large contingent of assault guards tried to wrest control of the Barcelona Telephone Exchange from the members of the anarchist trade union, the CNT. During the three days that followed, the streets of the city centre were the scene of the armed confrontations that eventually provoked the fall of Largo Caballero from power. Those combats, presented as an insurrection of fifthcolumnists organized by the POUM, were to justify the new government's actions against Nin's party. Between Juan Negrín's arrival in the presidency and the arrests of the POUM leaders, the Communist propaganda attacks grew worse against the 'Trotskyist agitators,' and *Mundo Obrero* labelled the organizations linked to the POUM as 'veritable guerrillas in our rearguard' and 'nests of fascists in the pay of German espionage rings.' With these accusations the ground was prepared for what was about to happen, and a very short time later, on 16 June, the POUM was banned and the members of its Executive Committee arrested.

From the information contained in the Alexander Orlov dossier, Catalan television journalists Dolors Genovès and

Llibert Ferri reconstructed Nin's murder in *Operation Nikolai*: his arrival at the Alcalá Prison, his refusal to confirm the accusations, the false rescue by members of the Gestapo... The names of the real kidnappers, all three of them Spanish, appear in the original of the dossier, but in the copy that was given to Genovès and Ferri only the initials are visible: L., A. F., I. M. took Nin from the prison and drove him to a nearby *cheka*. The *cheka* was located in a house that had been confiscated from its owners at the beginning of the war. Living in this house was Ignacio Hidalgo de Cisneros, head of the Republican Air Force and husband of Constancia de la Mora, who at that time was working in Valencia at the Foreign Press Office, and among her subordinates was Coco Robles. That was where Nin heroically resisted the torture sessions, imitating procedures then habitual in the USSR, intending to extract a 'voluntary' confession to facilitate the sentencing of the imprisoned POUM leaders.

In his book *The Spanish Civil War, the Soviet Union, and Communism*, Stanley G. Payne has revealed that Stalin himself hand-wrote the order (which is preserved in the KGB archives) to kill Nin. Stalin thus appears to be the one most interested in extending the climate of terror already prevailing in the USSR to Spain. The final sentencing of the POUM leaders for a few minor offences demonstrates the resistance by Republican institutions to Stalinist pressure. At the same time, the fate of the most outstanding Soviet envoys, whom Republican legal rights would be hard-pressed to protect, confirms that the storm of purges unleashed in the USSR extended in some measure as far as Spain. The ambassador, Marcel Rosenberg, was summoned to Moscow in February 1937 and was executed a short time later. His successor would be the Embassy counsellor, León Gaikis, who remained in the post for three months and would also be recalled to Moscow and executed. The same fate awaited other important members of the diplomatic legation, such as the commercial attaché Artur Stashevski or the consul general in Barcelona, Vladimir Antonov Ovseenko. Nor would the principal Soviet military advisors escape such an end, and among them was Yan Berzin, veteran of the 1905 and 1917 revolutions and former director of the GRU, and Vladimir Gorev (which led his companion and interpreter, Emma Wolf, to attempt suicide). The same thing would happen to the powerful correspondent Mikhail Koltsov (whose *Diary of the Spanish War*, partially published in 1938, was praised by Stalin and exalted by *Pravda* a few days before he was arrested and sent before a firing squad), and many others whose names have not been mentioned in this book. One of the few who did manage to get away with his life was the very man who had overseen the terror in Spain, Alexander Orlov, who, after being summoned to Moscow in July 1938, travelled to France to collect his wife and daughter, and from there managed to flee to the United States. The implacable Stalinist machinery imposed on its pawns the double role of victims and executioners, and in that way assured the maximum possible operational capacity. Everyone was suspicious in everyone else's eyes, and only by excelling in the mandatory repression of dissidence could they be confident of avoiding the effects of the terror, to which they would eventually succumb. Facing rivals like these, why would the POUM members think a better destiny lay in store for them than for the men convicted in the Moscow trials?

The brutal hunting-down of the supposed Spanish Trotskyists fed these fears. Testimonies can be found in the autobiographical books of the poet Stephen Spender, the literary critic Antonio Sánchez Barbudo, the writer Elena Garro, the painter Carles Fontserè... But surely the best known account is the one offered by George Orwell in *Homage to Catalonia*. Almost a week after the outbreak of the repression, the Barcelona newspapers (the only ones that made it to the Huesca front) had still not reported on what had happened. The POUM militias were still functioning as an independent unit, and at the front 'there must have been numbers of men who were killed without ever learning that the newspapers in the rear were calling them Fascists.' The militiamen who were on leave in Barcelona were arrested to keep them from returning to the front with the news, and the same fate seemed to await Orwell when, recuperating from his war wounds, he returned to the city after an absence of five days. His wife Eileen, whose hotel room had been thoroughly searched, was waiting for him in the hotel lobby and, as soon as she saw him appear, put her arm around his neck and whispered: 'Get out! Get out of here *at once*!' That is how he found out the party in whose militia he had enlisted to fight against fascism had been declared an illegal organization. He spent the following nights trying to sleep in the ruins of bombed-out buildings and tried to blend into the Barcelona crowds during the day. Wandering around, he constantly wondered why they were going to arrest him: What had he done? Eileen explained that it did not matter what he had or had not done: 'This was not a round-up of criminals; it was merely a reign of terror. I was not guilty of any definite act, but I was guilty of "Trotskyism". The fact that I had served in the POUM militia was quite enough to get me into prison.' After destroying the documents that linked him to the POUM, Orwell and his wife managed to cross the border. Neither of them ever knew how close they had come to danger. They left Spain on 23rd June, one day after the Negrín government published the decree creating the Special Tribunal for Espionage and High Treason. In a 1989 book called *The POUM Trial*, Víctor Alba brought to light the report prepared on the couple for that Tribunal. In the report, dated 13th July, their connections to the POUM and the ILP are documented, which means that if their escape had taken a little longer, nothing and no one would have saved them from sharing the misfortune of hundreds or thousands of their comrades.

Orwell was not the only one of the writers Dos Passos had met in Spain during the spring of 1937 who found himself in serious trouble. In *The Clash*, part three of the autobiographical trilogy *The Forging of a Rebel*, Arturo Barea remembers the implacable persecution he and his wife Ilsa were subjected to. At the end of 1936, when he had already joined the Press Department of the Foreign Ministry in Madrid, Ilsa travelled to Valencia, where she was arrested by 'an agent of the Political Police.' Having been denounced as a Trotskyist spy, she had to face a long interrogation, after which she was freed thanks to pressure from Rubio

Hidalgo. Some time later, the same agent who had arrested her warned them that Constancia de la Mora and Rubio Hidalgo had decided to dispense with her services and those of Barea, against whom there had been 'more than one complaint,' and replace them with a woman recommended by María Teresa León. By then, Constancia had taken control of the Valencia Press Office and was manoeuvring to free herself of the associates not to her liking, starting with Rubio Hidalgo. She advised Barea and his companion to take a long-overdue and much-needed vacation, and at first he did not suspect the sincerity of the offer. He only became aware of her true intentions when he received a letter informing him that this vacation had been converted into 'indefinite leave.' This happened in September 1937, and some time later, in a text dated 12th July 1940, collected in *Recovered Words*, Barea would claim that his dismissal had been a 'consequence of his silent struggle against the Valencia bureaucracy, in my opinion fascist under a revolutionary cloak.' Barea went straight back to Madrid and placed himself under the orders of General Miaja, and until November worked on radio broadcasts for Latin America, giving literary and propaganda talks as the 'Unknown Voice of Madrid.'

Around Barea, however, 'a tight net was closing in,' and vague accusations and suspicions against him and his companion began to circulate: 'Ilsa was either a Trotskyist and therefore a spy, or had committed imprudent acts, but anyhow she would shortly be arrested.' In spite of constant pressure, they resisted leaving Madrid until the day two police agents came to search their room. They didn't take much: his pistol, his small arms permit, some manuscripts, letters, photographs and... the signed copy of *The Forty-Second Parallel* that Dos Passos had given them when he visited the Press Office. In *The Clash*, Barea says they took it because Dos Passos 'had declared himself in favour of the Catalan POUM and the Anarchists.' That copy was the main piece of evidence they found to accuse the couple of Trotskyist sympathies, and the strange thing is that news of the episode reached Dos Passos before Barea related it in his book. In a July 1939 letter to Dwight Macdonald, Dos Passos tells him he has just found out about Barea's trouble getting out of Spain and adds: 'When the C.P. agents raided his room they found some Tauschnitz volumes I'd autographed for him and carried them off as evidence of Trotskyism (or whatever he was being charged with). It would all be comic in any other context.' Barea must have thought the same, as he wrote, 'I had sympathy neither for the POUM nor for their persecution.' His fragile nervous equilibrium cracked again, and Miaja granted him a special leave so he could go to Alicante to recuperate. He and Ilsa stayed for a month by the sea in San Juan, where they were picked up by SIM agents, and from there taken to Barcelona. They obtained permits to leave Spain, though not without difficulty, and, on the night of 22nd February 1938, five minutes before the permits expired, they crossed the border, where they had arrived in a police car after the one lent by the British Embassy broke down thirty miles from the frontier.

The story is yet to be told of the detentions of alleged Trotskyists after Negrín took over the presidency, and we have only the vague declarations like that of Orwell's wife, who had heard that in the first days of the repression they had arrested 'about four hundred in Barcelona alone.' But it seems obvious that such an estimation fell short of the truth, and Orwell himself rectifies it in the next line, saying 'I have since thought that even at that time the number must have been greater,' and that the arrests went on for months and swelled into thousands. The number of murders has not been established either and, although the majority of the victims were anonymous Spanish POUM members, the most widely reported were some illustrious foreign anti-fascists: the Czech Erwin Wolff, the Russian Marc Rhein, the British Bob Smillie, the Austrian Kurt Landau. Their names, together with Nin's, of course, served a group of foreign left-wing intellectuals to set in motion a campaign to demand a fair trial for the POUM leaders with full legal rights, a campaign to which not a single one of the principal figures of the Republican intelligentsia lent their support.

It is worth remembering the difficulties Orwell had in getting *Homage to Catalonia* published, after his regular publisher, Victor Gollancz, turned it down without even reading it, and the rough ride it had in the left-wing media: for the *New Statesman*'s critic, for example, his appetite for the unadorned truth was 'perverse.' The book's complete lack of impact, only selling a few hundred copies up till the end of the 1940s, speaks eloquently of Orwell's solitude in the defence of an anti-totalitarian vision within the left. In *Orwell's Victory*, Christopher Hitchens has written that, for the official left, the British author committed the definitive sin of 'giving ammunition to the enemy.' Undoubtedly, a similar accusation threatened (and gripped) Spanish intellectuals, especially at a time like that, in mid-1937, when the dominant rallying cry was 'first win the war.'

That the repression of the POUM was not even bloodier and more bitter was due to the fact that in the harshest moments, many anarcho-syndicalists of the CNT helped and sheltered them. They were not the only ones: Wilebaldo Solano remembers that, 'even during the time of clandestinity, there were Communist Party militants who warned us of what was about to befall us, who alerted us.' So the incendiary propaganda of those days, directly encouraging people to inform, did not always achieve its objectives, though certainly its principal message, repeated ad nauseum in the headlines, painted on walls and billboards all over Barcelona, and on the sides of buses, did manage to mobilize a large section of the Communist rank and file. The publications of the PSUC were exempt from censorship, but it took care of rounding off the task, diligently silencing any dissenting voices. Before such a panorama of informative intoxication, there were many honest anti-fascists who applauded the repression, when not actually contributing to it: why would they not accept the official thesis and justify the trials and imprisonment of the Trotskyist traitors who had incited rebellion in the rearguard to help Franco? And why should the reports coming from outside Spain be more believable than the reiterated messages of omnipresent and scarcely disputed propaganda?

It takes a wider stretch of the imagination to try to understand the motives that led certain revolutionary politicians and intellectuals, fully aware of the POUM's true nature, to collaborate in its annihilation. For that we need to reconstruct the image of the Soviet Union that had spread during the twenty years of its existence. The USSR had been born as the motherland of socialism and the proletariat, the country where a new world populated by new men was being forged, and which was developing a civilization without precedents. In that civilization, in contrast to capitalist societies, all evils would be resolved, and those who visited the USSR had the sensation of participating in an immense collective epic and living a radically new liberating utopia. The scientific character of Marxism, endorsed by the experience of the revolution of 1917, guaranteed the future victory of world revolution, to which every Communist wished to contribute. Pla wrote snidely of the Andreu Nin of 1925: 'when he talked about the society of the future, he got a little boring.' Those who killed Nin did so precisely in the name of that future society, in the name of that international revolution that seemed so close after the 'inevitable' triumph of Communism in Spain. But not only for that: also in the name of anti-fascism. Ever since Hitler's rise, the USSR had set itself up as the principal anti-fascist power, and its solitary support of the Spanish Republic made it legendary.

The most terrible thing about this story is that the victims and executioners of the Spain of 1937 shared the most essential thing: a Marxist faith in the future and the urgency to combat fascism. But for the executioners that was irrelevant beside the real question: the acceptance or not of orthodoxy, the submission or not to the dogma according to which whatever served the interests of the USSR (and, therefore, Stalin) was true and what damaged them false. Admitting this principle constituted the first step for all the rest: to justify the deficiencies in the construction of socialism, to tolerate the persecution of departures from the party line, to consent to crimes.

François Furet wrote in *The Passing of an Illusion*: 'Anyone who criticized Stalin supported Hitler. The genius of the Georgian was to have caught so many reasonable men in such a simplistic and formidable trap.' In the Spain of 1937 a great many reasonable men fell into that trap.

# NOTES

(Many of the sources for this book do not exist in English translations, but their titles have been translated within the text itself. The actual titles can be found in the bibliography.)

p1 **Dos Passos**, John Roderigo (1896–1970): Major 20th century American writer. A prolific novelist, playwright, poet, journalist, painter and translator, he is probably best known for the modernist, impressionistic novel *Manhattan Transfer* (1925) and his *USA* trilogy comprising *The 42nd Parallel* (1930), *Nineteen Nineteen* (1932) and *The Big Money* (1936).

The title of Héctor Baggio's book *John Dos Passos: Rocinante pierde el camino* is a play on the Spanish title of John Dos Passos' first book about Spain, *Rosinante to the Road Again*, which became *Rocinante vuelve al camino* in Márgara Villegas de Robles' translation.

p1 **Spanish Civil War**: War in Spain from 18th July 1936 to 1st April 1939. The country was very polarized after Spain was declared a Republic, for the second time, in April 1931. Elections held in early 1936 were contested by two broad coalitions: the Popular Front (an alliance of liberal and left-wing parties, ranging from social democratic Republicans to advocates of Basque and Catalan autonomy, socialists, Trotsykists and Soviet-allied Communists) and the National Front (supported by the conservative, fascist, Catholic and monarchist parties). The war broke out when a group of military officers, supported by elements from the right-wing parties, attempted a coup d'état to overthrow the Popular Front government but encountered resistance in Madrid and Barcelona. After numerous battles, the Republican forces were finally exhausted in 1939, and Franco declared the war over on 1st April 1939.

p4 ***Residencia de Estudiantes*** (Student Residence): Important Madrid cultural centre, founded in 1910. Well-known residents included Salvador Dalí, Luis Buñuel and Federico García Lorca.

p4 **Pío Baroja** (1872–1956): Spanish (Basque) writer who was a key member of the Generation of '98, a group of novelists, poets, essayists and philosophers in Spain during the Spanish-American War (1898).

p6 ***Institución Libre de Enseñanza*** (Free Institute of Learning): Founded in 1876 by a group of professors (including Francisco Giner de los Ríos and Gumersindo de Azcárate) expelled from the University of Madrid for defending freedom of expression and refusing to adjust their teachings to the official religious, political and ethical dogmas. See *Rosinante to the Road Again* (pp.104-106) for John Dos Passos' account.

p7 **Ramón del Valle-Inclán** (1866–1936): Radical and influential Spanish (Galician) dramatist, novelist, poet and member of the Generation of '98. His 1920 play *Divinas palabras* (*Divine Words*) is an indictment of greed, corruption and barbarism. His work has been compared to that of Bertolt Brecht and James Joyce.

p19 **GRU**: Russian acronym for the foreign military intelligence service.

p22 **Franco,** Francisco (1892–1975): General of the Spanish Army and one of the conspirators in the military revolt against the Republican government in July 1936, when he was stationed in Spanish Morocco. After an initial hesitation, he became the leader of the Nationalist forces during the course of the war. He ruled Spain as dictator from the end of the Civil War until his death.

p34 **Sacco & Vanzetti**: Nicola Sacco (1891–1927) and Bartolomeo Vanzetti (1888–1927), Italian-born American anarchist workers, executed in Massachusetts for an armed robbery and murder that they almost certainly did not commit. The case had a profound influence on the American left in general and on Dos Passos in particular, who mentioned or alluded to the men in several of his novels and other books. See especially *The Best Times* (pp.166-70) and 'The Wrong Set of Words' in *Travel Books & Other Writings* (pp.370-80).

p40 **PSOE**: The Spanish Socialist Workers' Party (*Partido Socialista Obrero Español*). Founded in 1833, it is one of the oldest and largest political parties in Spain, with strong links to the socialist trade union, the UGT (see below).

p42 **Montaña Barracks**: Army barracks held by the rebel General Fanjul, an ally of General Franco's, at the outbreak of the Civil War in Madrid. On 20 July 1936, thousands of citizens, among them police officers, soldiers and trade union members, attacked the Barracks. More than once soldiers inside tried to surrender by waving a white flag. The crowd approached the Barracks, while the surrendering soldiers were overwhelmed by the rebels, who opened fire with heavy machine guns and grenades on the advancing Republicans, leaving many wounded or dead. The crowd eventually stormed the Barracks and massacred most of its defenders.

p43 **Trotsky**, Leon (1879–1940): Russian political leader, prominent Bolshevik during the revolution of 1917 and creator of the Red Army. He lost influence after the death of Vladimir Lenin, when Joseph Stalin emerged triumphant from a power struggle. Trotsky was expelled from the Russian Communist Party and eventually from the Soviet Union. He was murdered by NKVD agents in Mexico.

p46 **CNT**: The National Confederation of Workers (*Confederación Nacional de Trabajo*). The main anarchist trade union, fighting for worker control of industry and agriculture, the CNT was particularly strong in Andalusia, Aragón and

Catalonia. Opposed to so-called representative politics, the anarchists supported none of the parties of the Popular Front but were among the first to organize militias to defend the Republic.

p46 ***Generalitat***: Regional autonomous government of Catalonia.

p54 **SIM**: The Military Investigation Service (*Servicio de Investigación Militar*). The political police organization created by Indalecio Prieto in August 1937, the SIM was almost immediately taken over by the Communists. It was a rationalization of the various intelligence services within the Republican forces. Previously the Army, the foreign ministry, the Catalan regional government, the Basque regional government in exile, the *Carabineros*, the International Brigades, etc., had each run their own counterespionage networks.

p56 ***Pravda***: Leading newspaper of the Soviet Union and official organ of the Russian Communist Party.

p61 **JSU**: The Unified Socialist Youth (*Juventudes Socialistas Unificadas*), a youth organization created in March 1936 by the union of the youth wings of the PSOE and the Spanish Communist Party (PCE, *Partido Comunista Español*), although leaders of the latter party held sway.

p64 See Stephen Koch, *Double Lives: Stalin, Willi Münzenberg and the Seduction of the Intellectuals* (NY: Enigma, 2003), pp.291-95. Note that in this book, Koch calls José Robles Pazos 'José Robles Villa.' Robles' son Coco (Francisco Robles Villegas) is also referred to as 'Robles Villa' while his wife Márgara is called 'Margare.'

Koch would go on to investigate the case more thoroughly, and shortly after the original Spanish publication of *Enterrar a los muertos* he published a book called *The Breaking Point: Hemingway, Dos Passos, and the Murder of José Robles* (NY: Counterpoint, 2005). While he gets the characters' names right in this recent volume, his basic hypothesis remains unchanged, i.e., that Herbst was a Comintern agent manipulating Hemingway and Dos Passos according to instructions from Moscow.

p70 **NKVD**: Soviet secret police. Precursor of the KGB.

p71 **Alexander Orlov** was known by many names over the course of his life. Born Leiba Lazarevich Felbin, he changed his name to Lev Nikolsky in 1920.

p71 ***chekas***: Improvised prisons in the Republican zone where justice was imposed by popular, revolutionary tribunals. *Chekas*, as the Russian-derived name suggests, were especially prevalent in areas controlled by Socialist or Communist parties or trade unions.

p72 **GPU**: Soviet secret police. Precursor of the NKVD.

p74 ***Regulares***: Volunteer infantry or cavalry units of the Spanish Army recruited in Spanish Morocco.

p75 **POUM**: The Workers' Party of Marxist Unification (*Partido Obrero de Unificación Marxista*). An allegedly Trotskyist party, it was founded in 1935 by Andreu Nin and Joaquín Maurín as a result of the merging of the Communist Left of Spain (ICE, *Izquierda Comunista de España*) and the Workers and Peasants Bloc (*Bloque Obrero y Campesino*), against the advice of Leon Trotsky.

p82 **UGT**: The General Workers' Union (*Unión General de Trabajadores*), one of Spain's largest trade unions, affiliated with the PSOE.

p86 ***Carabineros***: The border police force in prewar Spain. A majority of them remained loyal to the Republic after the uprising, fighting with the militias and later as an elite force within the popular Army.

p107 **FAI**: The Iberian Anarchist Federation (*Federación Anarquista Ibérica*), an anarchist organization linked to the CNT, dedicated to political activism.

p108 ***Esquerra Republicana de Catalunya***: The Catalan Republican Left, a left-wing political party founded in 1931 that campaigns for Catalan independence from Spain.

p153 See Constancia de la Mora, *In Place of Splendour: The Autobiography of a Spanish Woman* (London: Michael Joseph, 1940), pp.295-96. For some reason, de la Mora decided to leave this anecdote out of her own translation of her memoirs into Spanish.

p153 **'Poppy,'** according to Soledad Fox, was the American journalist Millie Bennett. See Fox's *Constancia de la Mora in War and Exile: International Voice for the Spanish Republic* (Eastbourne: Sussex Academic Press, 2007), p.186.

p157 **Juan Negrín** (1887–1956): President of the Government of Republican Spain from May 1937 to February 1939; Prime Minister of the Spanish Republican Government in Exile from 1939 to 1945.

p186 **Robles Piquer,** Carlos: Politician who held various important posts during Franco's regime, related by marriage to Manuel Fraga Iribarne, another prominent politician of the Franco era.

p205 **PSUC**: The Unified Socialist Party of Catalonia (*Partit Socialista Unificat de Catalunya*), founded in July 1936 by the unification of four left-wing Catalan parties, namely the Catalan branches of the PSOE and PCE, the Socialist Union of Catalonia (*Unió Socialista de Catalunya*) and the Proletarian Catalan Party (*Partit Català Proletari*).

# BIBLIOGRAPHY

ABRAMSON, Paulina and Adelina: *Mosaico roto*. Compañía Literaria. Madrid, 1994

AGRAMUNT, Francisco: 'La memoria oscura de las checas,' in *Historia 16*, nº 313. Madrid, May 2002

ALBA, Víctor: *Sísif i el seu temps*. Laertes. Barcelona, 1990

ÁLVAREZ DEL VAYO, Julio: *La guerra empezó en España*. Séneca. México D.F., 1940

ANDRADE, Juan: *Recuerdos personales*. Prologues by María Teresa García Banús and Pelai Pagès. Ediciones del Serbal. Barcelona, 1983

ANDRADE, Juan: *Notas sobre la guerra civil. Actuación del POUM*. Ediciones Libertarias. Madrid, 1986

AUB, Max: *Campo abierto* [1951]. Suma de Letras. Madrid, 2003

AUB, Max: *Campo de los almendros* [1968]. Alfaguara. Madrid, 1981

AYALA, Francisco: *Recuerdos y olvidos*. Alianza. Madrid, 1982

AZCÁRATE, Manuel: *Derrotas y esperanzas. La República, la Guerra Civil y la Resistencia*. Tusquets. Barcelona, 1994

AZNAR SOLER, Manuel, and SCHNEIDER, Luis Mario (eds.): *II Congreso Internacional de Escritores para la Defensa de la Cultura (1937)*. Generalitat Valenciana. Valencia, 1987

AZNAR SOLER, Manuel, et al: *València capital cultural de la República (1936-1937). Antología de textos i documents*. Generalitat Valenciana. Valencia, 1986

BAGGIO, Héctor: *John Dos Passos: Rocinante pierde el camino*. Altalena. Madrid, 1978

BAREA, Arturo: *The Forging of a Rebel*. Tr. Ilsa Barea [faber&faber 1941, 43, 46]. Granta. London 2001.

BAREA, Arturo: *Palabras recobradas. Textos inéditos*. Ed. Nigel Townson. Debate. Madrid, 2000

BLASCO, Ricard: 'Vida quotidiana,' in the catalogue of the exhibition *Valencia, capital de la República*. Ayuntamiento de Valencia. Valencia, 1986, pp.15-25

BONAMUSA, Francesc: *Andreu Nin y el movimiento comunista en España (1930–1937)*. Barcelona. Anagrama, 1977
BONET, Juan Manuel: *Diccionario de las vanguardias en España*. Alianza. Madrid, 1998
BONET, Juan Manuel: 'El surrealista errante. (Conversación con Eugenio F. Granell),' in *Syntaxis*, nº 16-17. Santa Cruz de Tenerife, winter-spring 1988, pp.135-158
BRONCANO RODRÍGUEZ, Manuel: 'José Robles Pazos: primer traductor de Dos Passos y Lewis,' in *Livius. Revista de Estudios de Traducción*, nº 2. León, 1992, pp.233-242
CANSINOS-ASSENS, Rafael: *La novela de un literato*. Alianza. Madrid, 1996
CARR, Virginia Spencer: *Dos Passos. A Life*. Doubleday & Company. New York, 1984
CASANOVA, Julián: *La Iglesia de Franco*. Temas de Hoy. Madrid, 2001
CASTRO DELGADO, Enrique: *Hombres made in Moscú*. Luis de Caralt. Barcelona, 1963
*Causa General. La dominación roja en España*. Prologue by Eduardo Aunós. Ministerio de Justicia. Madrid, 1944
COINDREAU, Maurice-Edgar: *Mémoires d'un traducteur. Entretiens avec Christian Giudicelli*. Prologue by Michel Gresset. Gallimard. Paris, 1974
COSTELLO, John, and TSAREV, Oleg: *Deadly Illusions*. Crown Publishers, Inc. New York, 1993
COY, Juan José: 'El compromiso ético en la literatura norte-americana,' in *Suplementos Anthropos*, nº 10, February 1989, pp.65-69
DOS PASSOS, John: *Rocinante vuelve al camino*. Tr. Márgara Villegas. Cenit. Madrid, 1930
DOS PASSOS, John: *Manhattan Transfer*. Prologue and translation by José Robles Pazos. Cenit. Madrid, 1930
DOS PASSOS, John: *Adventures of a Young Man* [1939]. Houghton Mifflin. Boston, 1967

DOS PASSOS, John: *In All Countries* [1934] in *Travel Books & Other Writings 1916–1941*. Compiled and annotated by Townsend Ludington. The Library of America. New York, 2003, pp.269-430

DOS PASSOS, John: *Un lugar en la tierra* [1951] in *Obras completas, II. Novelas*. Tr. Juan G. de Luaces. Planeta. Barcelona, 1957, pp.9-516

DOS PASSOS, John: *De brillante porvenir* [1954]. Tr. Carlos Peralta. Emecé. Buenos Aires, 1956

DOS PASSOS, John: *The Theme Is Freedom*. Dodd, Mead & Co. New York, 1956

DOS PASSOS, John: *The Best Times* [1966]. Andre Deutsch. London, 1968

DOS PASSOS, John: *Journeys Between Wars*. Constable & Company, Ltd. London, 1938

DOS PASSOS, John: *La Guerra Civil Española*. Prologue by Stanley Weintraub. Tr. Irene Geiss. La Salamandra. Buenos Aires, 1976

DOS PASSOS, John: *The Fourteenth Chronicle. Letters and Diaries of John Dos Passos*. Ed. Townsend Ludington. Gambit. Boston, 1973

DOS PASSOS, John: *Century's Ebb*. Gambit. Boston, 1975

EHRENBURG, Ilya: *Eve of War 1933–41*, Volume IV of *Men, Years, Life*. Tr. Tatiana Shebunina. MacGibbon & Kee. London, 1963

ELORZA, Antonio, and BIZCARRONDO, Marta: *Queridos camaradas. La Internacional Comunista y España, 1919–1939*. Planeta. Barcelona, 1999

ESTELLA, Gumersindo de: *Fusilados en Zaragoza. 1936–1939. Tres años de asistencia espiritual a los reos*. Mira Editores. Zaragoza, 2003

FERRI, Llibert: '"Nikolai": claror, ombra i penombra,' in *L'Avenç*, nº 166. Barcelona, January 1993, pp.34-37

FISCHER, Louis: *Men and Politics*. Duell, Sloan & Pearce. New York, 1941

FONTSERÈ, Carles: *Memòries d'un cartellista català (1931–1939)*. Pòrtic. Barcelona, 1995
FURET, François: *The Passing of an Illusion: the Idea of Communism in the Twentieth Century*. Tr. Deborah Furet. University of Chicago Press. Chicago, 1999
GARCÍA-ALIX, Carlos: *Madrid-Moscú. El cuento de nunca acabar*. T Ediciones. Madrid, 2003
GARRO, Elena: *Memorias de España, 1937*. Siglo XXI Editores. México D.F., 1992
GAZUR, Edward P.: *Secret Assignment: The FBI's KGB General*. St Ermin's Press. London, 2001
GORKIN, Julián (ed.): *10 novelistas americanos*. Zeus. Madrid, 1932
GORKIN, Julián: *La muerte en las manos. Novela del drama de España*. Prologue by John Dos Passos. Claridad. Buenos Aires, 1956
GORKIN, Julián: *El proceso de Moscú en Barcelona. El sacrificio de Andrés Nin*. Aymá. Barcelona, 1974
GORKIN, Julián: *El revolucionario profesional. Testimonio de un hombre de acción*. Aymá. Barcelona, 1975
GRANELL, Eugenio F.: *Ensayos, encuentros e invenciones*. Huerga & Fierro. Madrid, 1998
GUZMÁN, Eduardo de: *Nosotros, los asesinos*. G. del Toro. Madrid, 1976
HEMINGWAY, Ernest: *La guerra de España*. Prologues by Stanley Weintraub and Aldo Garosci. Tr. Carlos María Gutiérrez and Mario Schijman. Proceso Ediciones. Buenos Aires, 1973
HEMINGWAY, Ernest: *By-Line: Selected articles and despatches recording the adventure that was his life, and the events from which he fashioned his masterpieces*. Ed. William White. Collins. London, 1968
HEMINGWAY, Ernest: *Cuentos de guerra*. Tr. Félix della Paolera. Bruguera. Barcelona, 1980

HEMINGWAY, Ernest: *To Have and Have Not*. Charles Scribner's Sons. New York, 1937
HEMINGWAY, Ernest: *The Fifth Column and Four Stories of the Spanish Civil War*. Scribner's. New York, 1969
HEMINGWAY, Ernest: *For Whom the Bell Tolls*. Scribner's. New York, 1940
HEMINGWAY, Ernest: *A Moveable Feast*. Scribner's. New York, 1964
HERBST, Josephine: *The Starched Blue Sky of Spain and Other Memoirs*. Prologue by Elizabeth Francis. Northeastern University Press. Boston, 1999
HIDALGO DE CISNEROS, Ignacio: *Cambio de rumbo* [1964]. Ikusager Ediciones. Vitoria, 2001
HITCHENS, Christopher: *Orwell's Victory*. Penguin. London, 2002
HOBSBAWM, Eric: *Interesting Times: A Twentieth-Century Life*. The New Press. New York, 2005
IGLESIAS, Ignacio: *León Trotski y España (1930–1939)*. Júcar. Madrid, 1977
IVENS, Joris: *The Camera and I*. International Publishers. New York, 1969
KOCH, Stephen: *Double Lives: Stalin, Willi Münzenberg and the Seduction of the Intellectuals* [1994]. Enigma. New York, 2003
KOESTLER, Arthur: *Invisible Writing: Volume Two of Arrow in the Blue, An Autobiography*. Hamish Hamilton. London, 1954
KOLTSOV, Mikhail: *Diario de la guerra española*. Tr. José Fernández Sánchez. Akal Editor. Madrid, 1978
KOWALSKY, Daniel: *Stalin and the Spanish Civil War*. Columbia University Press. New York, 2004
LAFOZ, Herminio: 'Prisionero en San Juan de Mozarrifar,' in *Trébede*, nº 74. Zaragoza, April 2003, pp.45-47
LANGER, Elinor: *Josephine Herbst*. Little, Brown & Co. Boston-Toronto, 1984

LANGER, Elinor: 'The Secret Drawer,' in *The Nation*. New York, 30 May 1994, pp.752-757

LEÓN, María Teresa: *Memoria de la melancolía* [1970]. Bruguera. Barcelona, 1982

LEWIS, Sinclair: *Babbitt*. Prologue and translation by José Robles Pazos. Cenit. Madrid, 1931

LÓPEZ SOBRADO, Esther: 'Luis Quintanilla. Entre Santander y París,' in *Revista de Santander*, nº 61. October-December 1990, pp.37-43

LÓPEZ SOBRADO, Esther: 'El pintor Luis Quintanilla, espía en la Embajada,' in *Pluma y pincel*, nº 9. Santander, 2002

LUDINGTON, Townsend: *John Dos Passos. A Twentieth-Century Odyssey*. Carroll & Graff Publishers, Inc. New York, 1998

MACHADO, Antonio: *La Guerra. Escritos: 1936–39*. Ed. Julio Rodríguez Puértolas and Gerardo Pérez Herrero. Emiliano Escolar Editor. Madrid, 1983

MARTÍN GARCÍA, Eutimio: 'El turismo penitenciario franquista,' in *Historia 16*, nº 236. Madrid, March 1996, pp.19-25

MARTÍNEZ DE PISÓN, Ignacio: 'El periplo de Lydia Kúper,' in the *Culturas* supplement of the newspaper *La Vanguardia*. 4 February 2004

MARTÍNEZ AMUTIO, Justo: *Chantaje a un pueblo*. G. del Toro. Madrid, 1974

MEYERS, Jeffrey: *Edmund Wilson. A Biography*. Houghton Mifflin. New York, 1995

MEYERS, Jeffrey: *Orwell: Wintry Conscience of a Generation*. Norton. New York, 2000

MITCHELL, David: *The Spanish Civil War (Based on Television Series)*. Granada. London, 1982

MONTES, Catalina: *La visión de España en la obra de John Dos Passos*. Ediciones Almar. Salamanca, 1980

MORA, Constancia de la: *Doble esplendor*. Editorial Crítica. Barcelona, 1977

MORA, Constancia de la: *In Place of Splendour: The Autobiography of a Spanish Woman* [1939]. Michael Joseph. London, 1940
MORENO VILLA, José: *Vida en claro. Autobiografía*. El Colegio de México. México D. F., 1944
NEPOMUCENO, Eric: *Hemingway: Madrid no era una fiesta*. Altalena. Madrid, 1978
NOTHOMB, Paul: *Malraux en España*. Prologue by Jorge Semprún. Tr. José Carlos Cataño. Edhasa. Barcelona, 2001
OAK, Liston M.: 'Behind Barcelona Barricades,' in *The New Statesman and Nation*. London, 15 May 1937, pp.801-802
ORTIZ, Mauricio: *Del cuerpo*. Prologue by Antonio Tabucchi. Tusquets Editores México. México D.F., 2001
ORWELL, George: *Orwell in Spain*. Ed. Peter Davison. Penguin. London, 2001
PÀMIES, Teresa: *Quan érem capitans*. Proa. Barcelona, 1984
PARSHINA, Elizaveta: *La brigadista. Diario de una dinamitera de la guerra civil*. Tr. Dimitri Fernández Bobrovski. La Esfera. Madrid, 2002
PAYNE, Stanley G.: *The Spanish Civil War, the Soviet Union and Communism*. Yale University Press. 2004
PENALVA, Gonzalo: *Tras las huellas de un fantasma. Aproximación a la vida y obra de José Bergamín*. Turner. Madrid, 1985
PIVANO, Fernanda: *Hemingway*. Tr. Carmen Artal. Tusquets. Barcelona, 1986
PLA, Josep: *Viatge a Rússia el 1925* in *Obras completas. Volumen V*. Destino. Barcelona, 1967
PLA, Josep: *Homenots. Segona sèrie* in *Obras completas. Volumen XVI*. Destino. Barcelona, 1970
PRADO, Benjamín: *A la sombra del ángel. 13 años con Alberti*. Aguilar. Madrid, 2002
QUINTANILLA, Luis: *'Pasatiempo.' La vida de un pintor*. Ed. Esther López Sobrado. Ediciós do Castro. La Coruña, 2004
QUINTANILLA, Paul: *Waiting at the Shore (Art, Revolution, War*

*and Exile in the Life of the Spanish Artist Luis Quintanilla)*. Lulu Press. North Carolina, 2003
RADOSH, Ronald, HABECK, Mary R., and SEVOSTIANOV, Grigory (eds.): *Spain Betrayed. The Soviet Union and the Spanish Civil War*. Yale University Press. 2001
RAYFIELD, Donald: *Stalin and his Hangmen*. Viking. London, 2004
REYNOLDS, Michael: *Hemingway. The 1930s*. W. W. Norton & Company. New York, 1977
REYNOLDS, Michael: *Hemingway. The Final Years*. W. W. Norton & Company. New York, 1999
RIEGER, Max: *Espionaje en España*. Prologue by José Bergamín. Ediciones Unidad. Madrid, 1938
ROBLES, José: 'Libros yankis,' in *La Gaceta Literaria*, nº 8 (15 April 1927), 11 (1 June 1927), 18 (15 September 1927), 22 (15 November 1927) and 26 (15 January 1928). Topos Verlag Ag. Vaduz. Liechtenstein, 1980, pp.46, 64, 109, 132 and 162
ROBLES, José: *Cartilla Española*. F. S. Crofts & Co., Inc. 1935
ROBLES, José: *Tertulias Españolas*. Appleton-Century-Crofts, Inc. 1938
RODRIGO, Javier: *Los campos de concentración franquistas. Entre la historia y la memoria*. Siete Mares. Madrid, 2003
RODRÍGUEZ ESPINOSA, Marcos: 'Rusos blancos, bolcheviques, mencheviques y Trotskyists en la historia de la traducción en España,' in GARCÍA PEINADO, M. A., and ORTEGA ARJONILLA, E.: *Panorama actual de la investigation en traducción e interpretación*, Vol. II. Atrio Editorial. Granada, 2002, pp.65-73
ROJAS, Carlos: *Por qué perdimos la guerra*. Ediciones Nauta. Barcelona, 1971
RUBIO CABEZA, Manuel: *Diccionario de la guerra civil española*. Planeta. Barcelona, 1987
RUFAT, Ramón: *En las prisiones de España* [1966]. Ed. José Ramón Villanueva Herrero. Fundación Bernardo Aladrén. Zaragoza, 2003

SALAZAR CHAPELA, Esteban: *En aquella Valencia*. Ed. Francisca Montiel Rayo. Biblioteca del Exilio. Sevilla, 2001

SALINAS, Pedro, and GUILLÉN, Jorge: *Correspondencia (1923 –1951)*. Ed. Andrés Soria Olmedo. Tusquets. Barcelona, 1992

SÁNCHEZ, Germán: 'El misterio Grigulévich,' in *Historia 16*, nº 233. September 1995, pp.115-122

SÁNCHEZ BARBUDO, Antonio: *Ensayos y recuerdos*. Laia. Barcelona, 1980

SANTONJA, Gonzalo: *La República de los libros. El nuevo libro popular de la II República*. Anthropos. Barcelona, 1989

SANTONJA, Gonzalo: *Los signos de la noche. De la guerra al exilio. Historia peregrina del libro republicano entre España y México*. Castalia. Madrid, 2003

SENDER, Ramón J.: *Casas Viejas*. Prologue by Ignacio Martínez de Pisón. Prensas Universitarias de Zaragoza. Zaragoza, 2004

SENDER, Ramón J.: *Álbum de radiografías secretas*. Destino. Barcelona, 1982

SHERIDAN, Guillermo: 'Un no en Valencia,' in *Letras libres*, nº 24. Madrid, September 2003, pp.12-17

SOLANO, Wilebaldo: *Vida, obra y muerte de Andreu Nin*. Ed. Vicente Álvarez. Barcelona, 1977

SOLANO, Wilebaldo, and FERRI, Llibert: *Diàlegs a Barcelona*. Ayuntamiento de Barcelona. Barcelona, 1994

SPENDER, Stephen: *Un mundo dentro del mundo*. Tr. Ana Poljak. Muchnik. Barcelona, 1993

STEPANOV, Stoyan Minev: *Las causas de la derrota de la República española*. Edited and translated by Ángel L. Encinas Moral. Miraguano. Madrid, 2003

TODD, Olivier: *André Malraux. Una vida*. Tr. Encarna Castejón. Tusquets. Barcelona, 2002

TRAPIELLO, Andrés: *Las armas y las letras. Literatura y Guerra Civil (1936–1939)*. Península. Barcelona, 2002

VAILL, Amanda: *Everybody Was So Young. Gerald and Sara Murphy: A Lost Generation Love Story*. Broadway Books. New York, 1999
WILSON, Edmund: *Letters on Literature and Politics. 1912–1972*. Ed. Elena Wilson. Prologue by Daniel Aaron. Preface by Leon Edel. Farrar, Straus & Giroux. New York, 1977
WILSON, Edmund: *The Thirties*. Ed. Leon Edel. Farrar, Straus & Giroux. New York, 1980
ZUGAZAGOITIA, Julián: *Guerra y vicisitudes de los españoles*. Tusquets. Barcelona, 2001

Other documents:

*José Robles Pazos Collection*, collection of letters and documents in the Milton S. Eisenhower Library at Johns Hopkins University (Baltimore)
*The Papers of John Dos Passos*, in the Alderman Library at the University of Virginia
Collection of letters from John Dos Passos to José Robles, courtesy of the Ortiz Robles family
Procedimiento sumarísimo de urgencia nº 620/38 (Francisco Robles Villegas) del Juzgado Togado Militar Territorial nº 32 (Zaragoza)
Service Record of General Ramón Robles Pazos (*Archivo General Militar*, Segovia)
José Robles Pazos' handwritten applications deposited in the Archive of the *Residencia de Estudiantes* (Madrid)
Declarations from the archive of the *Causa General* (*Archivo Histórico Nacional*, Madrid)
Collection of newspapers from the Civil War at the *Centre d'Estudis Històrics Internacionals* (Barcelona)
Collection of newspapers in the *Hemeroteca Municipal de Madrid* and the *Biblioteca de Catalunya*

KURZKE, Jan, and MANGAN, Kate: *The Good Comrade* (unpublished memoirs)
AZCÁRATE, Luis: unpublished memoirs

# INDEX

## PHOTOS AND ILLUSTRATIONS

# ACKNOWLEDGEMENTS

I'd like to dedicate this book to the memory of Miggie Robles (1924–2006), without whose generous collaboration it would have been a different and, of course, worse book.

Also to José Luis Melero and Félix Romeo, my habitual interlocutors but especially during the time it has taken me to write this book.

There are other people and institutions who have facilitated my research: Francisco Agramunt, Cristina Allott, Asunción Almuiña, General Archive of the Spanish Civil War (Salamanca), General Military Archive (Segovia), Luis Azcárate, María José Belló, Alderman Library of the University of Virginia, Biblioteca de Catalunya, Milton S. Eisenhower Library at Johns Hopkins University (Baltimore), Juan Manuel Bonet, *Causa General* (Archivo Histórico Nacional, Madrid), Ricardo Cayuela, *Centre d'Estudis Històrics Internacionals* (Barcelona), Carlos García-Alix, Fernando García-Mercadal, Fundación Andreu Nin, Hemeroteca Municipal de Madrid, Juzgado Togado Militar nº 32 (Zaragoza), Charlotte Kurzke, Esther López Sobrado, Mónica Martín, Anne McLean, Antoni Munné, Mauricio Ortiz, Mario Ortiz Robles, Javier Rodrigo, Germán Sánchez, Antonio Pérez Lasheras, *Residencia de Estudiantes*, Andrés Trapiello and Juan Villoro. To all of them, many thanks.

The caricature of Álvarez del Vayo and the photo of Dos Passos with Liston Oak are, respectively, the work of Maside and Agustí Centelles. The drawings by José Robles are from his book *Tertulias Españolas*, except for the one that illustrated his review of *Manhattan Transfer* for *La Gaceta Literaria*. The title of the Carlos García-Alix painting is 'Los invisibles (María Cristina Bar).'

I have chosen to spare the reader of this edition the abundant notes, which scholars wishing to check details and sources can consult in the original Spanish edition.

IMdP

The translator would like to thank Colin and Harriet Ward for their help and advice, and Ignacio Martínez de Pisón for gracious elucidations and endless patience.

AM